TALK BEAUTY TO ME

TALK BEAUTY TO ME

HOW MARKETERS CAN SPEAK THE LANGUAGE OF BEAUTY TO THE NEXT GENERATION

KANIKA MALAVIYA

NEW DEGREE PRESS

TALK BEAUTY TO ME
How Marketers Can Speak the Language of Beauty to The Next Generation

ISBN   978-1-64137-012-7 *Paperback*

978-1-64137-016-5 *Ebook*

CONTENTS

INTRODUCTION...3

CHAPTER 1: YOUTH TO THE PEOPLE...........................15

CHAPTER 2: BEAUTY FOR ME.......................................27

CHAPTER 3: BEAUTIFUL RIGHTS, STRONGER TOGETHER.......39

CHAPTER 4: SAVE OR SPLURGE....................................51

CHAPTER 5: ALL-IN-ONE...65

CHAPTER 6: MODERN MEDIA.......................................77

CHAPTER 7: NEW SPEECH..91

CHAPTER 8: PERSONALIZED CONCENTRATE.................101

CHAPTER 9: UP THE AMP...113

CHAPTER 10: SHOW & TELL..127

CHAPTER 11: BACK FOR MORE......................................139

CHAPTER 12: FRESH FACE...153

CHAPTER 13: EVERLASTING BEAUTY.............................167

ACKNOWLEDGEMENTS...173

"It's quite fun to do the impossible."

— WALT DISNEY

INTRODUCTION

———

"Can you guys help me pick a filter?
I don't know if I should go with XX Pro or Valencia
I wanna look tan
What should my caption be?
I want it to be clever
How about "Livin' with my girls, Hashtag live"
I only got 10 likes in the last 5 minutes
Do you think I should take it down?
Let me take another selfie."

— #SELFIE BY THE CHAINSMOKERS.

What, exactly, is a selfie?

selfie, *n.* 1. self-photo usually taken with a mobile phone and posted online to social media sites.

The word was officially added to the Oxford Dictionary in 2013. Today, nearly everyone — from celebrities to average Joes — takes advantage of smartphone cameras and photo-editing apps to show off their lives in style.

With that, we have firmly entered the age of the #selfie.

Although this book isn't about selfies, they're a good place to start when analyzing the habits of the tech-savvy, social media-obsessed, millennial generation.

The first use of the selfie hashtag appeared on Flickr in 2004, but it took over a decade for the masses to jump onto the bandwagon.

The original selfie hashtag has grown more than 200 percent in usage between 2013 and 2017, without even being one of the top tags used on Instagram.

And the use of #selfie doesn't stop at just the general population. Did you see Ellen DeGeneres' 2014 Oscar selfie? Talk about #squadgoals. I mean, let's be honest, without the self-promotion of celebrities in pop culture, millennials would have much less to talk about.

A recent study by Now Sourcing and Frames Direct reveals some surprising statistics about selfies. For instance, Instagram has almost 250 million #selfies to date, with millennials making up 55 percent of those posts. The study predicts the average millennial will spend about an hour a week taking selfies. At that rate, some have the potential of taking up to 25,700 selfies in their lifetime.

The study also shows that millennials spend an average of seven minutes on each selfie. In those seven minutes, millennials take the selfie, edit the selfie, realize their lipstick looks bad, take the selfie again, edit the new selfie, and then decide on a caption after the approval of at least three friends.

"What emoji should I use? Maybe adding a hashtag would be cute".

There are clearly a lot of decisions made in those seven minutes.

But why do millennials even bother?

To start off, let's determine who millennials are.

The millennial generation consists of people born between 1982 and 2004 and was given its name for being born at the dawn of the 21st century — the new millennium. Millennials are characterized as highly educated, career-driven, politically progressive, and, contrary to popular belief, have the ability to develop strong brand loyalty when presented with quality products and active engagement by brands.

Why do companies care so much about millennials? Collectively, millennials are expected to spend significantly more than previous generations with over $200 billion annually in 2017 and $10 trillion in their lifetimes. They are gaining influence over older generations as trendsetters in all industries, ranging from fashion to food.

As the first to be born into a digital world, millennials are often associated with the internet and social media, and more specifically the practice of incorporating social media into daily life. This demographic group is one of the heaviest media users, some of whom, according to IDG Media, will click, tap, or swipe on their phones over 5,427 times a day!

As a millennial, I would say that at a surface level, I take selfies because they are a way to capture memories with friends and show my followers what I'm doing. But if I honestly ask myself why I take selfies, it's to promote "Brand Kanika." For the longest time I always thought my personal brand was entirely determined by me, but I've learned that, in reality, my personal brand is influenced by what other people think once I leave the room. I could think I'm the most energetic and talkative person in the world, but to others, that sociability may come off as self-centered. First impressions are unavoidable and made in a blink of an eye, so rather than letting others be the judge, I want to have at least some control of their perceptions by showing them what I believe best represents me. I post on social media to help others have a particular notion of who I am.

I'm not the only one who thinks this way. Dr. Terri Apter, a professor of psychology at Cambridge University, says taking selfies is all about trying to figure out who you are, and then projecting that vision to other people. "It's a kind of self-definition," says Dr. Apter. "We all like the idea of being sort of in control of our image and getting attention, being noticed, being part of the culture."

Since the rise of portraiture in the 15th century, "people who had access to self representations were keen to make use of them," Apter says. "In this way, people could control the image projected, and, of course, the fact that the image was on display, marked the importance and status of the person represented" — which is exactly what I realized my own motives were.

Most of my peers agree that it's all about being in control of their own image. It's much easier to edit and control the way you look in a selfie than it is in a picture someone else takes of you. After all, a picture is worth a thousand words. So we all want to put forth the best words we have about ourselves.

The ability to pick and control your own look is exactly how selfies on platforms like Instagram and Twitter are changing the face of beauty retailing.

According to Investor's Business Daily, more than nine million posts on Instagram get the tag #selfiesunday, over six million are marked #selfienation, about 275 million are tagged #selfie, and 302 million are simply tagged #me.

With all these selfies being taken every day, you'll start noticing products like Makeup Forever's "HD Foundation" and PÜR Cosmetic's "Love Your Selfie" palette while you're browsing the aisles at Sephora.

Coincidence?

Not at all.

Camera-friendly beauty products are the result of millennial influence on makeup. These cosmetics are now standard products sold at specialty beauty stores like Ulta Beauty and Sephora. As Amazon continues to rake in more dollars from consumers, brick-and-mortar chains are quickly turning to the social media-driven craze for cosmetics and skin care products, which are proving to be a sliver of hope for a wide range of stores trying to lure in Instagram-savvy shoppers.

As a result of this push from millennials, specialty retailers are integrating in-store digital experiences to present consumers with the gadgets and technologies they already gravitate toward in their daily lives, attempting to appeal to their consumers' combined love for beauty and obsession with technology and media.

That brings me to my reason for writing this book:

Millennials are misunderstood and generalized.

According to Gloria Roheim McRae, Senior Solutions Consultant at HootSuite, "the problem is not with millennials; it's in expecting us to pursue an outdated, one-size-fits-all approach to the North American dream. There will be disappointment if we are expected to fit our square peg selves into that round hole. The world has changed. We've been told to get a good education, get a good job, get married, buy a home, have babies, raise kids, collect our pension, and then we've earned the right to live. We inherited this dream map from our parents, from our school system, and from portrayals in the media. This may have suited our parents' generation. However, I would assert that judging by divorce rates and the decline in pension security, that it didn't fit them all that well either. Alas, it is to this that we say, 'no thank you' and we are misunderstood for it."

Millennials are nothing like previous generations. They want what McRae calls "a modified North American Dream," or "N.A.D. 2.0." According to her, millennials want to be self-sufficient and financially independent from their parents. They value their freedom, family, and community, and desire a lifetime of contribution. "And yes, [millennials] can value all that and still enjoy taking selfies at every turn. [They] are redefining how [they] achieve the dream, in what order, and what [they] do along the way."

McRae herself realized she wanted more freedom and social purpose in life, rather than a five-figure salary, a condo, and two degrees. After she sold her condo, ended her relationship with her boyfriend, and quit her job, many people called her entitled, impatient, and ungrateful.

"I worked damn hard to get to where I was, and I did so trusting the conventional road to the North American Dream," she says. "While I did that, I ignored my deep-seeded desire to chart my own course toward my dreams. I was raised to know my worth and to believe that anything is possible if you put your mind to it. That's when I chose to pivot. Fast-forward five years. I turn 29 this year, met and married the man of my dreams, I am a proud entrepreneur of my second company ... [and an author]. I'm free, more fulfilled than ever, and self-sufficient. I don't own a condo or car now, but so what?"

McRae's story does a perfect job of clearly showing how

millennials have a completely new and different mindset compared to that of their parents. They want different things, and therefore, when considering product consumption and marketing, one can assume they want marketers to talk to them much differently than they talked to their parents.

Yet the internet is filled with article after article complaining about millennials, especially in fashion and beauty magazines.

"7 Reasons Why Millennials Are The Worst Generation"

"Millennials: The Me, Me, Me Generation"

"Millennials and 'Their Destruction of Civilization'"

Like McRae, I've experienced this misunderstanding myself.

There is a common assumption that millennials are indecisive. I'll admit that I find it hard to make decisions. I always want to be sure I make the best decisions to avoid the regret of wishing I had acted differently. I constantly seek out the help, advice, and guidance of others. I can count the number of times I have made a decision on my own without asking even one other person, or without having an internal battle with my "angel and devil".

My current Facebook profile picture, while not a selfie, was sent to several group chats and had back-and-forth exchanges to get the approval of my closest friends before posting and sharing it with the world. I needed to get verification from others to be sure that they wouldn't judge me negatively for what I was doing.

I don't want to disappoint myself or others, which can easily be viewed as indecisiveness. But I disagree.

The underlying reason behind my inability to pick a side, and indeed much of the perceived indecisiveness of millennials, results from growing up with choices for just about everything we have ever needed or wanted, more so than for any previous generation. As a result, we view life differently and thus want to be reached differently as consumers.

As McRae demonstrates, millennials haven't grown up plotting their life path. The one that has been followed by my own family for generations is pretty straightforward: go to school for a bachelor's, master's, then a doctorate degree; get married; raise a family; live a well-off life; and finally retire and watch your grandkids grow up. Although I have stuck to this path so far, as a millennial, I recognize that this isn't the only path available to me.

According to Patrick Spenner, a strategic initiatives Leader in CEB's Marketing practice, millennials see limitless possibilities for their lives, which is often why they are called narcissists or assumed to be in a perpetually stunted state of adulthood. But in reality, many aspects of adulthood that were common among previous generations, like those noted by McRae, are not as desirable to young people as they were in the past. And, more importantly, millennials simply know they have a lot more options and alternatives to pick from when creating their own adulthood.

The problem with articles complaining about false perceptions of millennials is clear: those making the broad generalizations do not tend to be millennials. But who would know millennials better than millennials themselves? So, I turned to my friends, family, peers, beauty influencers, and experts to help me speak for my generation as to what millennials need to see from marketers in the cosmetics and beauty industries.

Millennials aren't difficult to market to; they're different to market to.

Millennials are overwhelmingly frugal and make decisions only after consulting a variety of sources, from friends to media to online reviews. They care about products that are good for them and the environment. They do care about how they look, not just to influence others' perception of them, but also for themselves to engage in "me-time" and "self-care." And contrary to popular belief, millennials are also loyal to brands — even if to a fault.

So, I want to shed light on the reality of why millennials are the way they are, like the things they like, and act in the way they act. I want to show that marketing to millennials is simple once you understand their true motives, especially with regard to self-image and appearance.

Millennials have redefined what it means to market in the beauty industry. They post every single detail of their lives on social media, so they're certainly not trying to hide from brands. They simply have different values, beliefs, and opinions compared to those of their parents and grandparents. And, I believe these differences actually make this generation one of the easiest to reach from a marketing standpoint. Let me share with you why.

CHAPTER 1

YOUTH TO THE PEOPLE

———

"Beauty preparations were passed down from mother to daughter."

— MARK TUNGATE, AUTHOR OF BRANDED BEAUTY:
HOW MARKETING CHANGED THE WAY WE LOOK.

Like many others her age, 14-year-old Megan puts on makeup nearly every day as part of her usual routine. But Megan stands out from other typical cosmetics users by recording her makeup routine and posting it on YouTube for her 18,000 followers. Megan, also known as Meggs and Bacon, is one of thousands of bloggers offering beauty and lifestyle tutorials to followers. But what makes her especially unique is her narrator: her 42-year-old dad, Jon.

Instead of narrating the video herself, Megan has her dad offer the step-by-step commentary as she paints her face.

"OK," says Jon. "First I'm gonna use, this is Elf hydrating moisturizer, and it's made — it's actually a primer — it's made from the sweat of elves, and it's very expensive."

In the now viral video, Megan holds up her Elf hydrating primer to the camera, a $6 steal from the brand whose name isn't referring to fictitious woodland creatures, but actually stands for Eyes, Lips, and Face.

She continues on with her routine, holding up CoverGirl's Clean Sensitive Skin Liquid Foundation and dabbing it on her face before blending it in with a BeautyBlender sponge.

Jon continues to chime in, mostly obliviously: "I use this little egg that's squishy, and you just have to dab, dab, dab. And what I like to do is make silly little spots. It's kind of like makeup camouflage. So if there's a whole bunch of makeup around you, you wouldn't be able to see me, because I'm camouflaged."

While most beauty tutorials may have just a couple thousand views, Jon and Megan have broken the mold with more than 2.3 million views in Megan's "Everyday Makeup Routine" tutorial as of May 2017.

**

Much like Megan, and many others, my interest in beauty,

was sparked — or in some ways un-sparked— by my parents. Certainly, many women have gotten their first exposures to makeup from their mothers.

The first lipstick I tried on was my mom's. The same goes for my first foundation, blush, eyeliner, and moisturizer. The first thing I ever learned about beauty and cosmetics was from her. I used the knowledge she gave me and grew up putting my own spin on it, creating greater and more elaborate works of art.

My "approved" introduction to makeup came earlier for me than for some of my friends because of one of my favorite hobbies: dance.

Even as young 7-year-old girls, we were expected to wear makeup for recitals, so I would show up ready to go, with a full face of makeup on. Of course, at that age, I had no idea how a tube of lipstick worked, let alone how to apply it.

"Kanika!" My mom would say as she saw me twisting the tube higher and higher. "You've broken my last four lipsticks. Here, let me show you how to do it," she would say, taking the tube out of my hand.

My mom always did my makeup for me before my shows. She would sit me down at her vanity, and I would watch her in the mirror to see what she was doing. She would gently brush blush on my cheeks, explaining to me how to apply it and why people used it. Then she would grab some lipstick and slowly apply it to my lips.

Like most girls that age, I would be fascinated by how different I looked when my mom was done applying my makeup. I would sit at the mirror pursing my lips and turning my cheeks from side to side to admire the blush until she would call my name, signaling that it was time to leave for my recital.

As the years went on and the recitals went by, I would sit at her vanity and let her start the process. Before she could finish though, I would grab the next product and start applying it myself. I would start digging through her other makeup and ask her how to use that too. I loved how much you could do with makeup, how you could create whatever look you wanted with just a few products, and how the look would completely change based on how you used each of them, whether by applying more or less of the product, or by hacking products like blush and eyeshadow, by using them for multiple purposes.

Eventually, I would do it all by myself. Fifteen minutes before I would need to leave for my recitals, my mom would call my name throughout the house, frantically looking for me to make sure I was ready. She would find me sitting at her vanity, doing my own makeup.

My initial lipstick brand was Revlon, the brand my mom uses. Of course, I've changed colors — I couldn't wear the bright-red shade I wore on stage everywhere I went — and even added a new brand as my go-to primary shade I carry with me in my purse. But I still always have at least one stick of that red Revlon tube that my mom first introduced me to when I was being made up for my dance recitals.

Today, like my peers, I'm grown up, out of my parent's home and away from that first influence — my mother — on my beauty and makeup routine. Yes, my routines are colored by my mother and her lessons, but I am no longer seated in her vanity, learning from her.

According to the Boston Consulting Group's 2013 Global Consumer Sentiment Survey, which surveyed over 800 millennials, while parents are still influential, friends and celebrities are playing increasingly important roles in influencing their buying decisions.

"Millennials reported that they are influenced the most by family, friends, and strangers. Asked to name the type of people who influence their purchasing decisions, 59 percent of millennials listed friends — compared to less than half of non-millennials. Of the millennials, 52 percent cited spouses and partners, and 51 percent cited parents; 33 percent, roughly twice as many as non-millennials, listed strangers, and 23 percent cited celebrities. Millennials were twice as likely as Gen-Xers to say that they are influenced by celebrities, four times more likely than boomers, and ten times more likely than Silents. Indeed, the influence of celebrities on millennials appears to have increased, especially when it comes to apparel, lifestyle, and luxury categories and brands."

Look no further than beauty vlogger Megan, who garnered 2.3 million views on a single video, which had incredible product placement for each and every make up product she used. In a world where technology is on the rise, digital and social media are becoming key influencers on consumers.

Let's be honest: there is no exact way to market a product. You have to be creative, innovative, and different. Trends are constantly changing, and therefore, customers never want to see and hear the same things over and over again.

This is especially true in the beauty and cosmetics industry, since everyone's definition of beauty is different across the world, and everyone has different needs when it comes to products.

I'm sure you've heard the saying "beauty is in the eye of the beholder," and, now more than ever, this is true. Millennials' buying habits are changing the beauty industry.

Influencers like Megan — and the other 50 plus million millennials who themselves serve as influencers on their friends — are changing the face of marketing, in terms of reach, relevance, reputation, relation, and referral.

These are the five Rs, each of which represents a new challenge for marketers trying to engage a generation that approaches brands differently than any previous one:

- Reach
- Relevance
- Reputation
- Relation
- Referral

Reach. This generation doesn't necessarily look for brands; they expect brands to come to them. They are engaged in more media and technology than older generations, which means they are constantly bombarded with ads no matter where they are or what they are doing.

Relevance. Millennials are the hardest to convince that a brand is relevant. They will only pay attention when they feel information could be useful to them. For instance, regardless of how relevant a product itself may be to me, I will not turn to the product unless the brand resonates with me, too. There are many consumers in the market, and if I see the product marketed or broadcast in a way that doesn't appeal to me individually or match what I am looking for, I will immediately be turned off by it.

Reputation. Today, shoppers tend to identify more with brands on personal and emotional levels. They look for brands that they can relate to and those whose values and status align with their own so that they have a reason to stand behind the brands and products they use.

Relation. To stay loyal to their brands, millennials rely on establishing relationships with them. They want to have personal, timely, and straightforward interactions with their brands, just like any other relationship they would have with a real person, and they want to be heard at any time and place.

Referral. Finally, millennials value referrals and opinions. They want to research products before making purchases, and they do so by look for reviews. Personally speaking, my decision to purchase a product is more heavily influenced by my peers than by the company itself. This means that not only do others have the power to influence me, but I have the power to influence others. This makes these consumers an immensely powerful tool in terms of marketing and brand communication.

What ties all five of these factors together?

Quite simply: **trust**

This is why the millennial generation values the opinions of those closest to them. They trust the experiences of others and make a lot of their decisions based on what they have to say, relying on reviews to make most of their purchase decisions. Millennials look through reviews not only on the retailer's website, but also on wholesale sites that also sell the product, on blogs, and they will even ask friends what they think of the product. This creates a multi-leveled sales process that is often hard for marketers to narrow down to a pattern.

"Compared to other generations, millennials tend to be more collaborative," says author Joanie Connell in her book *Flying Without a Helicopter: How to Prepare Young People for Work and Life.* Connell writes that millennials are more willing to work with and rely on others for help, which is why they turn to each other even when purchasing products.

As an essential component of this trust, millennials value **authenticity**.

If consumers don't trust the retailer, there is no way that brand can convince them to buy one of its products. Go online and search for your favorite product — then go to a grocery store or corner store. Does it look the same in both places? Judging by those comparisons, shoppers will pick certain retailers and brands over others.

Millennials want to know that the brands they shop with are up-front and truthful about the products they are selling. Have you ever seen those clothing sites that sell clothes at such a low price that you question how they're able to even make a profit? BuzzFeed posts like "Here's Why You Should Think Twice Before Clicking On That $12 Dress On Facebook" show that a $12 dress is too good to be true by presenting side-by-side comparisons of what clothes look like online versus when they come in the mail.

Millennials are turned off in instances when promises aren't held and their expectations don't match reality. After an experience like the one in the BuzzFeed article, a consumer might choose to shop in stores, or if shopping online, could decide to purchase from well-respected stores like Zara and Madewell, instead of sites like Zaful, Shien, or Fashionmia.

Once Millennials form opinions about brands, whether good or bad, they will stick to their judgement. Millennials are loyal to brands, meaning they are more likely to buy from brands they have already purchased from and have had good experience with, because they are more likely to trust them.

I buy all my jeans from American Eagle, all my sneakers from Nike, and all my devices from Apple. None of these brands have failed me yet, so I don't have a reason not to purchase from them.

And I'm not alone. This individual loyalty is why marketing to millennials has become such a challenge to companies, especially in the beauty world. When it comes to beauty products, everyone's needs are different in very nit-picky ways, from the color of a lipstick all the way down to the way it glides when being applied to the lips, and how it feels once on.

Beauty Tips:

- The use of digital and social media is rising to become a key influence on consumers.
- Millennials don't necessarily look for brands, but rather, they expect brands to reach out to them.
- These consumers need to be convinced that a brand or product is relevant to them before they will consider spending their time and money on it.
- Millennials connect with brands on personal and emotional levels, seeking to align their personal values, beliefs, and mission, with the brands they associate with.
- Relationships are crucial . Consumers want their brands to be committed and engaged, which will help ensure their loyalty.
- Millennials go out looking for the referrals and opinions of those

they trust the most in order to get more information about products and services.

- Trust is the foundation on which you need to build on to speak to this generation.

CHAPTER 2

BEAUTY FOR ME

---

*"If you deal with every customer in the same way, you will only
close 25 to 30 percent of your contacts, because you will only
close one personality type. But if you learn how to effectively
work with all four personality types, you can conceivably close
100 percent of your contacts."*

— ROB NICHOLS, FORMER PROFESSIONAL BASEBALL PITCHER
WITH THE CLEVELAND INDIANS, LOS ANGELES DODGERS,
AND ATLANTA BRAVES, AND AUTHOR OF "SUCCESSFUL
NETWORK MARKETING FOR THE 21ST CENTURY".

"Kelly, you're so lucky to have straight hair. It always looks
amazing. I don't think I've ever seen you having a bad hair
day," said Mallory as the three girls slowly inched their way
to their history lecture, the most dreaded part of their day.

"Are you kidding?" Kelly replied. "My hair can't even hold a curl. I literally can't do anything with it besides leave it straight."

"Well, at least it doesn't get frizzy when it rain or gets humid," Olivia inserted. "My hair turns into a wild creature in the summer. No matter what product I use, nothing helps."

"Wow, that's so different from my hair. No matter what type of product or brand of product I use, my hair will always become so greasy that I need to wash it twice in the same day," Kelly said. "I used to use the OGX Coconut Milk Anti-Breakage Serum all the time, until I realized it left my hair really oily. I haven't used any product in my hair ever since."

"Wait really?" Olivia asked. I use that all the time. It makes my hair soft and shiny, while repairing any split ends I have from all the heat damage from my straightener."

"Same," Mallory agreed. "I need to use product in my curls to tame them a little."

As they kept talking, the three girls made it to class with seconds to spare before the professor started the lecture.

**

There are over 7.5 billion people on this planet, out of which

92 million are millennials. Each individual millennial in this generation is different — with different wants, needs, desires, and preferences that all shape their individual shopping habits.

When it comes to beauty, I have met three very different types of consumers: the makeup enthusiast, the daily user, and the occasional user.

The Makeup Enthusiast:

Imagine the typical beauty blogger. She knows all the ins and outs of makeup. She is your go-to if you have any questions about beauty, from general to specific. She has every type of product out there, for any purpose, and she knows exactly how to use them all. She's the girl who has every edition of the Naked palette, and who buys the new Kylie Lipkit before it sells out the first time. She loves makeup and has a passion for it.

Meet Bella, an enthusiast, who has my dream Instagram account and whose blog I scroll through in my free time. She sees beauty as less of a hobby and more as a part of her life.

What is your definition of beauty?
Without being cheesy, I really think that beauty comes through when someone is happy with both their self and their appearance. I've seen pretty girls in gorgeous, expensive makeup that don't radiate beauty, and I have

friends who wouldn't know concealer from mascara who look beautiful every time I see them. I think your own self-esteem determines the beauty you effuse; makeup or product isn't always a part of it. For me personally, I only feel comfortable with my appearance when I'm wearing makeup, so my "beauty" — which I correlate with my self-esteem and self-value or worth — is inherently dependent on me being comfortable with how I look. It might not be the healthiest or ideal lifestyle, but everyone is different. While I am fully aware that my appearance is far from the only thing that defines me, I know for a fact that I am not the only person who correlates their self esteem with their appearance in this manner; we are undoubtedly a marketing team's dream customers.

What got you interested in beauty? Why is beauty such a big part of your life?

I think that, as a millennial, I'm a member of a self-obsessed society. Selfie culture has completely changed the way we view ourselves, and our self-worth has begun to increasingly be defined by our appearance, our aesthetic, etc. Investing in beauty is a quick fix for those imperfections that stare back at us in our iPhone front-facing cameras. And because marketing companies are able to target these insecurities and use them as tools through which they can grow interest in brands, the beauty industry is now bigger than ever before. For me personally, beauty is an art form. I love creating and experimenting with products, and I consider my beauty routine as much of a hobby as it is a dependency. However, not everyone feels this love for beauty, and many women instead feel obligated to participate in beauty culture so as to live up to society's unreasonable expectations for female appearance.

What do you specifically look for when buying beauty/ cosmetic products?

The top three would be promotion, packaging, and performance. I'm a devout watcher of lots of members of Youtube's beauty guru community, and I follow a myriad of Instagram pages dedicated to hauling, swatching, and reviewing products. When there seems to be a lot of buzz about a particular product — regardless of whether it occurred organically or as the result of a strong marketing effort — I make a mental note to consider purchasing the product for myself. This is also where packaging comes in, which also goes back to being a member of the Instagram age. Aesthetic matters, so packaging that appeals to me makes me more eager to test out a product I otherwise might not notice. Finally, performance is what keeps me coming back to a product. Marketing can only be so impactful if the product itself doesn't end up living up to the hype. I've fallen for a million wonderful marketing campaigns about specific beauty products, only to test them myself and wonder why that hype was so fabricated.

What is the one thing you believe has the greatest influence on you when buying products in terms of marketing?

Personalization. Whether it's a serum specifically made for my skin type or lip products that adapt and color-match according to my pH, the more catered it is to my specific needs, the better. Unsurprisingly, as a member of the "me, me, me, generation," I gravitate towards products that are marketed as custom. It's rare that the same beauty products work for everyone, as we all come with different skin types, skin tones, and coverage preferences.

The Daily User:

Imagine the girl who puts on makeup as she is running out the door in the morning. She has perfected the "no-makeup" look and uses fewer than five products on a daily basis. She is able to transform her day-to-day look into her night look with a little mascara and lipstick. She enjoys using makeup and gets a kick out of putting it on for special occasions.

That's me, the girl who loves makeup but likes to keep things simple.

What is your definition of beauty?

Beauty is relative. To me, beauty can be anything you want. Everything can have beauty and be beautiful. Beauty is the perfect combination of elements that create an aesthetically pleasing image.

What got you into beauty?

From a young age, I have been into art. I grew up painting, drawing, and doing pottery. To me, using beauty products was the same, with my face and body as the canvas. I loved to create art, whether it be bright red lips, bold smokey eyes, or subtle nude nails. Growing up, I was also always curious. I always wanted to experiment and see what look different combinations of products could create. I would mix together two or three lip sticks or layer different lipsticks with lip glosses. There was always something that I wanted to test out.

Why is beauty such a big part of your life?

I'm going to go ahead and say it: it's because of the expectations created by the media. My day-to-day makeup routine takes not even five minutes, with just some concealer, bronzer, and mascara, but I still do take that time to cover up anything that is considered "imperfect." However, I would say that the reason why beauty takes up such a big part of my life is because it's fun! It's fun to get made-up when I'm going out to dinner. It's fun to get pampered for a special occasion. I'm one of those people who likes to keep things simple but always enjoys adding a little more when the opportunity presents itself.

What do you specifically look for when buying beauty/ cosmetic products?

When buying products, I look at trust and quality. I'm personally not the type of person who is willing to spend $40 on the new Chanel foundation. I would much rather stick to my $10 Maybelline concealer from CVS that has been doing the job for the past four years. It's a product that hasn't failed me yet, so I have no reason to use something else. However, that doesn't mean I'm not the type to give up quality. I have tried countless drugstore face cleansers that were just not working for me. Now, I swear by Shiseido, and I wouldn't dare try anything else. I learned that some-times, quality trumps quantity.

What is the one thing you believe has the greatest influence on you when buying products in terms of marketing?

When looking at the marketing, I think the beauty claims have the biggest influence on me. If something says it's extra long-lasting, moisturizing, or brightening, I will fall for it and believe it.

The Occasional User:

Imagine the girl who knows as little as possible about makeup. She walks into Sephora with the intention of buying some type of foundation before a formal, but she ends up walking out with foundation, concealer, and three types of brushes because the sales associate convinces her she needs everything for just the one night. She uses makeup, but rarely. When she does, it takes her about 30 minutes to put on eyeliner, before she even realizes she still has the other eye to go.

Meet Brittany, who barely uses makeup.

What is your definition of beauty?

When I think of beauty, I think more of being internally beautiful; someone who is nice, a good person, and caring. I think that when you exude that, it turns you into an attractive individual. I know that in society today, beauty is made and created with the help of products but I personally don't think anyone needs makeup or anything to enhance their beauty. I think beauty comes naturally from a person, not a product. That's why I barely use any myself. I think it's important for us to all embrace our natural beauty rather than cover it up with products.

What got you into beauty?

I take pride in how I present myself and my appearance, but for me beauty is both inside and out. Of course, I try to be fit and have a good appearance, but I also think it is important to be a good person, meaning kind and caring.

Why is beauty such a big part of your life?

My definition of beauty is important to me because our relationships and interactions with others are so crucial and important. It's really important to keep good relations with others and, I know this is cheesy, but it helps make the world a more beautiful place. I look for beauty in everything and everyone, regardless of what others think.

What do you specifically look for when buying beauty/ cosmetic products?

Since I only use makeup once in a while, I look for something that is inexpensive, easy to apply, durable, and performs well on my sensitive skin. The occasional time I do use makeup is if I'm going out with friends, for business events, or just special events in general. Even for those events, I keep it really minimal. I just stick to eyeliner, mascara, and maybe something subtle on my lips. When I buy products, I look for those that are also "nutritious" and good for my skin. For example, the mascara I buy is strengthening mascara because I know that using mascara on your lashes weakens them, so I make sure the products don't detract or negatively affect my skin when I do use them.

What is the one thing you believe has the greatest influence on you when buying products in terms of marketing?

Well, for beauty products in general, since I don't really use them too much, my mom has had the biggest influence on which ones I use. She introduced me to Neutrogena for all the basics, and I've been sticking to those as my core products. I do also turn to my friends, because I am a little helpless when it comes to makeup. If I see that I like their eyelashes, I will ask them what product they are using and will be more inclined to check it out next time I am at the store. I also look for the benefits of the products, by which I mean if it's "long-lasting" or "strengthening." The packaging is also a big thing for me. If it looks nice and natural, it is more appealing to me. Since makeup is not really something I think too much about, I am easily influenced by the basic marketing techniques that someone would tell you to never fall for.

These three millennials all have unique backgrounds, beliefs, and preferences, and, are therefore, not influenced by the same factors. It is essential that all marketers who are reaching out to this generation are aware of these differences and truly find the best way for their brand to attract and retain their target consumer. It's all about the marketing and image that these brands are putting forth to shoppers.

Beauty Tip:

- Every millennial is different — consumers in the beauty industry are all unique and have their own preferences based on a variety of factors, ranging from how they were raised to how society has shaped their values and beliefs.

CHAPTER 3

BEAUTIFUL RIGHTS, STRONGER TOGETHER

"Millennials will soon have the greatest purchasing power of any demographic and their mindset is influencing how women of all ages shop."

— JANE HERTZMARK HUDIS, ESTÉE LAUDER
GROUP PRESIDENT, WHO OVERSEES SIX
BRANDS INCLUDING ESTÉE LAUDER.

"Hey, pass me the eyeshadow. What color do you think I should try today?" Mary asked as she turned away from the mirror toward her friends in the school bathroom.

"I think blue would look good with your outfit. What do you think, Emily?" Sarah replied as she finished applying her lip gloss.

With one eye lined and the other bare, Emily picked up the eyeshadow palette from the sink and carefully looked at all the colors she had to pick from. "Yeah, I think blue would be perfect," she said, as she handed the palette over to Mary, and went on to apply the liner to her second eye.

"I never thought to try the blue before. Are you guys sure it would look good?" Mary nervously questioned, as she picked up her eyeshadow brush and dabbed it on the light blue color located in the center of the palette.

"Are you kidding? Of course it will look good. Avril Lavigne wore it on the red carpet last night! If she wore blue eyeshadow, it's definitely going to become a trend," Emily said, before even giving Mary a moment to think about what she was doing.

"Well, that's enough to convince me," Mary laughed, as she turned to the mirror and swept the blue onto her eyelids.

"BEEEEEP," the buzzer signaling the start of first period resounded through the school.

"Quick, we have five minutes to get to class!" The girls rushed to finish applying their makeup and threw everything into their bags. They took one last look at themselves in the mirror, making any last minute touch-ups with their fingers, then quickly ran out of the bathroom with a minute to spare.

⁎⁎

The first thing I did when I got to school in 7th grade was head straight to the bathroom with my friends to put on makeup. At the time, I associated wearing makeup with being older and more mature, so I wanted to be able to use it as soon as possible. I would drag my mom, who had to accept that girls were putting makeup on at earlier stages of their lives, to CVS and try to get her to buy me every possible product on the selves. I am proud to say that at one point I had every Smuckers lip gloss flavor available.

Millennials have a purchasing power unlike that of any previous generation. When they set their minds to something, they will do anything in their power to have things their way.

Growing up, my mom told me I wouldn't be able to buy my own makeup and wear it to school every day until I was in college. She didn't let me get my eyebrows done until I was in high school, at which point they were out of control.

"Mom, can you *please* buy me some?" I would beg her as I walked by a window display of Smuckers lipgloss at the mall.

"No, not today," she would reply every time, like it was an automatic response just waiting for the question to be asked. "You'll get your chance to wear makeup when you're older," she would tell me, as she dragged me away from the store.

My mother believes in natural beauty — she wants me to let my skin breathe rather than have it entirely covered by chemicals. I, however, do not completely agree with her, most likely because of the influence of my peers.

However, this desire to use makeup is what has given my generation a growing importance in the global beauty market. According to the Millennials and Beauty report by Fung Global Retail & Technology, the global cosmetics market increased by 3.9 percent in 2015, with category sales reaching $375 billion at retail prices. In the next 10 to 15 years, as millennials start entering into the job market, allowing them to earn and make money, their spending power will increase, and the cosmetics market is expected to double in value.

With this growing influence, millennials are transforming the beauty industry by redefining which products are most important to them as consumers. Now more than ever, there is a shift towards focusing on well-being and a rise in the concern for one's wellness. Millennials are generation "treat yo' self ", demonstrating a need for an increased sense of self-care and of self-worth by using all-natural and organic products.

In her article, *Hygge Beauty: Future Trend?*, Jennifer Sain, from the Center for Marketing Intelligence identified "2016 [as] the year of hygge in the US. Hygge, to simplify, is the Danish concept of enjoying the good, simple things in life and is often associated with coziness. It evokes feelings of well-being and balance, and while it is most often associated with the winter months, it carries into warmer days, as well."

"So, what does this all have to do with beauty?" She goes on. "Well, Mintel recently suggested that the feelings hygge stirs in consumers may have strong implications for the beauty market. Furthermore, GCI writes that 'brands that put a focus on rituals, aromatherapy, and enjoyment of products in order to inspire purchases will be well on their way to 'hygge-ing' the lives of consumers.'"

"In line with hygge's focus on pleasure, beauty products are an accessible and affordable way of treating oneself and can be perceived as a means of self-care. Mintel says that the subscription box market, especially, presents an opportunity 'to send hygge to consumers,' with its potential to create an experience. Combining candles and beauty products, such as comforting creams, with food and drink can create very hyggeligg moments. Opportunities also abound for spas and salons to appeal to consumers with hygge themes, creating social treatment evenings such as gathering with friends and loved ones, is also a key component of hygge."

On Instagram, #selfcare has well over a million posts, including images of sliced persimmons, clay face masks and many yoga poses. #SelfcareSunday joined #Throwback-Thursday, #MotivationMonday, and #FlashbackFriday as some of the most commonly used hashtags on social media.

Millennials' beauty perceptions are very different from those of older generations. Younger consumers are much more likely to buy all-natural cosmetics than older generations. During the last decade, skin care was the dominant segment in the industry, while fragrances were facing a decline in usage. But today, fragrances are outperforming skin care; skin care and wellness are merging into the same category; and the lines are blurring between skin care and makeup.

Consumers believe they are able to have a direct impact on their own health, as well as the health of the environment, by purchasing these products. Women are reading product labels just as closely as food labels, scanning for ingredients they want to avoid. They are looking at skin care as an extension to their health. As a result, beauty counters are getting cleaner. The global organic personal care market is expected to reach $25.11 billion by 2025 with cosmetics-generated revenues exceeding $2 billion in 2015, according to a new report by Grand View Research Inc.. This has resulted in an increasing number of companies striving to connect with consumers by leveraging organic or natural chemicals and products.

I remember a few years ago, I was on the hunt to find the right skin care products for myself. I was trying on so many different products with harsh active ingredients, like salicylic acid and benzoyl peroxide. I will admit, I was never the best at reading labels, but my mom always told me to never eat food with ingredients that I couldn't pronounce, and I applied that to my skincare search too. Using these active ingredients dried out and irritated my skin. After doing some research, I found Shiseido's Pureness line, which is made without any added alcohols, and instead, uses natural ingredients, like beeswax and rosemary extract.

The first question I asked Georgia Garinois, executive vice president of corporate marketing at The Estée Lauder Companies Inc., was how the company is balancing the differing wants and needs of its thousands of consumers all around the world. She told me Estée Lauder strives for what Fabrizi Freda calls, "creativity-driven and consumer-inspired vision." The company focuses on identifying consumer insights, then analyzing data in order to marry consumer power with brand equity, to truly match the needs of its consumers and present them with products they want. At the same time, the company is still able to stay true to the brand's mission and values by not giving its consumers too much influence.

My peer Natalia, who now works at La Mer in their global marketing department, talked to me about being consistent with brand image but still taking risks. For example, snail-based skin creams are popular in Korea. However, the problem La Mer faced when trying to expand to that market was that the product didn't align with the company's offerings products and message to "heal your skin." Instead, the brand introduced an aqua peel, which it is marketing as a gentle skin-peel mask. This shows the importance of incorporating the trends that work best for the company, regardless of what consumers are demanding. It is crucial to not hand them too much power since they are not afraid to takecontrol. Brands still need to stay true to their base foundation.

With this in mind, companies are reworking their marketing strategies. Underdogs, such as Kari Garn, a mineral makeup brand that sells all-natural products with simple and natural ingredients, are rising in popularity. The company stands on the the motto "be kind to your skin," with the mission to nourish skin to help it meet its most basic needs. After all, skin is the largest organ, and it faces the most daily wear and tear.

Tarte Cosmetics is another major brand that sells products that, although are not all-natural, are a lot "cleaner" than most competitors. Tarte creates cruelty-free and ecofriendly products. The company has products that are hypoallergenic, soy-free, and vegan-friendly. Not only that, but Tarte also has a variety of philanthropic projects, so every purchase goes toward doing good for the planet, its people, and even its animals.

Unilever's chief marketing and communications officer, Keith Weed, is trying to conform to this trend. "To break through the clutter and get noticed has never been so hard," he told his audience at the Cannes Lions Festival of Creativity. "As a solution, Unilever is approaching brand stories differently by incorporating broader messages into its campaigns. Rather than listing the product advantages, for instance, a Seventh Generation campaign features comedian Maya Rudolph singing a humorous jingle about chemicals in feminine products. People want to care about things rather than sell a product," Weed says.

According to Omnicom Group's Cone Communications, 70 percent of millennials will spend more on brands supporting causes they care about, making social responsibility a considerable priority to brands targeting this group of shoppers.

My friend Mallory is very passionate about the environment and cares a lot about how we are living on our planet. When it comes to "organic" and "all-natural" products, she says that she definitely prefers these types of products:

"I like that using clean and natural products eliminates some of the harm our planet experiences. Clean products are a great idea, and I try to get them often. But I don't buy them as frequently as I want to because I am a college student and such products tend to be far more expensive than others. But it is something I keep at the back of my mind and consider before purchasing my products."

Millennials are redefining what it means for beauty retailers to sell their products by shifting away from what baby boomers valued the most. For the last 10 years, it's been all about lines and wrinkles. Millennials are simply less worried about the lines, the wrinkles, and the gray hair. They want their appearance to be more natural to enhance those features, rather than cover them up. This growing group of consumers is posing a threat to how companies have become accustomed to marketing. Now, companies have to learn to navigate their way through this period of change.

Beauty Tips:

- Millennials have purchasing power and are willing to take advantage of that. They are willing to share their voice and are confident they can create the change they need to get what they want.

- Understanding who your consumers are and knowing what they are looking for is the key to success. Preferences change and, therefore, it is essential to keep up with growing trends.

- By looking for natural products, millennials are moving away from what previous generations wanted, and instead, are asking for products to be as clean and as harmless as possible.

- Millennials care about causes. It's not just how the products can benefit the consumer, but how they can benefit the environment around them.

CHAPTER 4

SAVE OR SPLURGE

———

"Who's going to pay $50 for a blowout?"

— JESSICA RICHARDS, FORMER VOGUE EDITOR
AND CURRENT OWNER OF SHEN BEAUTY,
A BEAUTY RETAILER IN BROOKLYN.

"Hi, how much is it for a gel manicure?… $40? Okay, thank you."

Carla hung up the phone and scrolled through her Google search results for the next nail salon on the list. She dialed the number and was once again disappointed by her conversation.

"$45?… Thank you, have a good day." Her search wasn't getting any better. As a college student, Carla just wanted to find a good deal for a gel manicure. She was losing hope but remembered one more salon that she thought she could try.

"You said $25?... Do you have anything available in about 15 minutes .... Okay, perfect, I'll see you soon."

**

Who would pay $50 for a blow out or $45 for a manicure? I mean I sure wouldn't. I don't even spend the extra $6 when I get a haircut for them to blow dry my hair at the end. Simply said, I, along with many other millennials, am price conscious.

Millennials spend less on beauty than other groups because they tend to make less money. What might be surprising, though, is that they are more likely to buy more units of beauty products. According to a 2015 report from TABS Analytics, consumers ages 18 to 34 account for about 47 percent of heavy buyers of beauty, or those who buy over 10 products out of a possible 19 categories. Now that's a lot.

This is because millennials look for deals. They are always bargain hunting and looking for ways to get more bang for their buck. I'll admit it: I'm frugal when it comes to any type of shopping, especially while I'm shopping for beauty products. When I'm buying something I need, like my go-to Maybelline mascara, I will look at CVS, Rite-Aid, and Walmart before making my final purchase. Even though the difference is only a couple of dollars, I would rather spend less than more. Thirty-nine percent of my fellow millennials would do the same — they use coupons when purchasing personal care products to save where they can.

The problem with bargain hunting in the beauty industry is that it doesn't happen as often with high-end and luxury products, such as MAC and Clinique. But then how do these companies still manage to convince this generation to buy their products?

Companies can accomplish this through two main tactics: establishing a personal relationship with their customers and controlling the perception of quality of their products.

Today, consumers are willing to share private information with retailers to form deeper connections and allow them to better understand the consumer they are selling to. This allows companies to create **personal relationships** with their customers, which they can then use to encourage buyers to purchase more expensive products.

**

"Guys, we need to leave before we are late! Dad already left in the other car," Carla called to her sisters, trying to get them out of the house as fast as possible.

"We're coming, Carla! Calm down! Do you have the keys?"

asked her sister Camille as she headed for the door.

"Yes, come on, get in the car," Carla said, losing her patience.

Carla and her sisters, Camille and Bianca, were headed to Tiffany & Co. to get their mom a Mother's Day gift. It's the only jewelry store Carla could remember having an emotional connection to. Growing up, their mom always bought them gifts from Tiffany's, and, once they could afford it, Carla and her sisters always went on Mother's Days to get their mom a present. It became a family event.

The family members were such frequent customers that they built connections and relationships with specific sales associates who always helped them while they were in the store.

"Oh, how nice it is to see you again!" Serena, the associate, exclaimed, greeting Carla and her family as they opened the tiffany blue doors and walked into the store lined with glass displays. Serena ran over to hug them all.

"It's been so long since we last saw you," Camille said, "We're back for another Mother's Day gift. Do you think you could help us find one as good as last year's?" "Well, of course! Come this way. I put aside a special selection just for you," Serena said, as she directed the family to a counter at the center of the store.

∗∗

Just like Carla and her family, millennials want to go back to the places they have deep and meaningful connections with. When Carla thinks of Tiffany's, she thinks of it as being simple, glamorous, high-end, timeless, and reliable. She has been able to create a deep and meaningful personal relationship with the brand, which is something she never wants to lose.

To help form these relationships with brands, millennials are more honest and vocal about their desires, and they are willing to work with retailers to tell them exactly what they want. The Millennials and Beauty report by Fung Global Retail & Technology found that 60 percent of millennials are willing to provide details about their habits and preferences to marketers so they can understand them better. If it means a better shopping experience and higher overall quality, consumers are open to sharing, hoping for a certain level of quality from the brands they trust. In return, millennials expect the brands to match, if not exceed, the standards they were promised.

I am constantly filling out online forms and questionnaires asking me for feedback, which I'm always willing to give, whether it be good or bad.

I don't know about you, but when I get those emails from Amazon after I buy a product asking me for a "quick favor" regarding my "experience so far with a new item," I will usually take the 30 seconds to give my review. Ever since I was able to get $30 back after receiving a used textbook that was supposed to be in "new" condition, but in reality was falling off it's binding, I have always taken advantage of opportunities to give feedback. I have a friend who went to go watch a movie and complained about a purple circle that appeared on the bottom left of the screen for the entire time, and got free tickets as a courtesy.

Millennials are willing to be open and honest with their brands and are not scared to share or talk about their experiences.

The second reason millennials will spend more is because of their **perception of quality** of the brand, which then becomes a question of what's worth it and what's not. Millennials want to spend more to indulge, but when does that indulgence become too much?

We see the Kardashians snapping their multi-step makeup routines that require at least 10 different products.

We see celebrities' makeup artists constantly sharing the products they use and recommend the most.

We see countless DIY makeup tutorials all over the internet.

Simply put, there are so many cues pointing toward so many different products. It becomes overwhelming! I know when I walk into a Sephora, I feel like I walked into a Forever 21. I need to go in with a game plan, because otherwise, there is no way I can spend more than five minutes in there before I lose my mind.

With so many available products on the shelves, where is the limit on what to buy?

To indulge is to allow oneself to enjoy the pleasure of something.

For my friend Carla, jeans have become something she found she needed to indulge in by spending a little more to get the quality she wanted out of them.

"I'm so picky about my jeans," she said. "I went through so many different brands: Old Navy, Abercrombie, Forever 21 — the list goes on. But then, one day, I found TopShop. Even though those jeans are way more expensive than what I used to buy, I got them because they are a lot more comfortable and durable. I've worn them practically every day for the past two years, and I'm just going back today to get new ones!"

And for her it's not just the brand, but it also has to do with the retailer it sells through.

"I shop at Nordstrom, which already has a great reputation for caring about its customers, along with the qualityofthe products sold. The fact that TopShop introduced its clothing in Nordstrom stores already gave its brand a leg-up in my mind. When I tried on the jeans, they were perfect. They were exactly my style and they had lots of options, something that I felt was always limited with other brands. I bought the jeans on the spot. They looked amazing on me, so I was like 'Yeah, I have to get them.' Today, it's not so much that I'm indulging; it's more like I'm just replenishing my stock. TopShop jeans have been part of my life for years now, and they are an item that I need in my wardrobe."

Like Carla, I used to indulge in getting a gel manicure after a stressful week or a hard exam. But over time, the indulgence has turned into a necessity. I now get my nails done every two weeks, regardless of what else is going on in my life. I can't stand it if my nails are not done, which goes to show how perceptions change. A simple indulgence turned into an habit that can't be broken anymore.

However, what millennials and older generations consider a necessity can be very different. My mom, for example, will never spend money on a manicure or pedicure. For many years now, I have tried to convince her otherwise, but our conversation will usually go like this:

We will both be sitting on the couch in the living room with the Food Network on, when I turn to her and say, "I'm going to get my nails done. Do you want to come with me? My treat!"

Every time I ask, she will turn to me and say, "I'll do your nails for you. Run upstairs and pick a color from my vanity. You don't need to spend money on something you can do yourself!"

"But mom, it's not the same! I'm getting a gel manicure, not a regular one!" I'll whined back.

"You need to let you nails breathe. You always have them painted. It's not natural." She'll automatically reply.

Then I'll roll my eyes and say, "You work so hard. You should get them done as a relaxing reward! Just come with me. It'll be fun," as my attempt to change her mind.

At this point my dad would overhear the entire conversation from the other room and would say, "Just go with her! It'll be some nice mother-daughter time."

"No, even if I get them done, they will start to chip right away because I do so much work around the house. I'll go with you if you want but I don't want mine done," she would reply back, at which point I roll my eyes again.

My mom simply doesn't see her nails as something important to take care of. She would rather spend her money on groceries, clothes, and bills — things that I haven't had to worry too much about, yet. But I do know that even when I am living off of my own income, I will still be setting aside $60 a month for two gel manicures, something my mom has never, and will never, do.

When looking at the extensive number of products available, it's easy to indulge. Just think of a time you walked into Sephora and bought what feels like about half the store.

"Oh, I've done that so many times. It gets kind of concerning. I'll walk [into Sephora] with the intention of buying just one thing, but then I see so many products that I've heard about and have been considering trying, or that I use and know I'll need to replenish eventually, so I just buy them. Next thing I know, I've just spent my entire paycheck the day after I got it. I generally try to save money and am not the biggest spender, but once in a while I think it's necessary to indulge."

That's my roommate Avery. She knows way more about how to use makeup than I ever will. She knows exactly how to apply every product and the specific brush you need for it.

She uses "natural lighting" when applying her makeup, since it's the best lighting for it. She knows what works best for her skin and is even able to make suggestions for others. Simply said, she loves and wears makeup every single day.

Another easy place to lose your senses and let your guard down is when shopping online. I know I've done this, as often-times I'll be scrolling down a page only to realize I already looked at it. My mind just goes blank and my heart does the shopping for me. I'll be scrolling through all of a company's products and all of a sudden, I have about 15 things in my cart. And luckily — or unfortunately — my credit card information is already saved on the site and in a matter of five seconds, before I can even process anything that's going on, I've just spent over $200.

Of course, after about 10 minutes I'll start trying to justify my purchase and say, "Oh, I needed all those things," or "It was a good deal, and there's no way I could pass it up." Essentially, I tell myself I indulged and, since it doesn't happen that frequently, it's okay.

This is where quality also comes into play. Millennials are willing to spend a little more if it means purchasing a trusted, high-quality product that meets all their needs.

I know that the products that I'm going to indulge in are

going to be worthwhile. The way I see it, if I'm going to spend, I might as well spend on high quality, well-reviewed products that I find appealing. For me, indulging can even be buying a brand-name product over the generic — it's more trusted and has a higher perception of quality, since it is tied to the brand and the larger ideologies associated to it though advertising, reviews in the media, or celebrity endorsements. When I buy Neutrogena makeup wipes, I think of Hayden Panettiere, whereas if I go for the cheaper CVS brand, I simply think of a pharmacy.

But, all in all, it's give and take. We all have our preferences. I know I'm willing to indulge a little more when it comes to skin-care, but there's no way I'm going to spend $30 for bronzer if I can get the exact product I need for half the price with Physicians Formula from CVS.

That being said, I know a lot of people might disagree with me when I say I see nothing in the hype behind the Kylie Lipkit. Long before the products were even launched, I found NYX Matte Lip Cream — only $6. When the Lipkit first came out, I was definitely interested in the products, but $29 was not a number I could justify, since it was a lot more than I had ever spent on something for my lips.

When my roommate bought the Lipkit, I tried it on, but was slightly disappointed. It completely dried out my lips and was not really what I was expecting from a high-end product. I was happy with my $6 drugstore product, and I knew that not spending my money on the Lipkit would allow me to spend more money on products I actually believed were worth it.

What's worth it and not worth it is different for everyone. Since Millennials are more price conscious than earlier generations, they rely more on budgets and try to save money where they can. Some will spend more on certain products over others, but this is simply because they all have their own individual wants and needs that they are trying to fulfill.

Beauty Tips:

- Millennials are price-conscious. They constantly try to cut costs and save money where they can.
- These consumers are willing to share private information with retailers to receive a more personalized shopping experience.
- Building personal relationships with millennials allows you to speak to them at a more intimate and one-on-one level that fosters a sense of commitment to each other.
- Consumers like to take advantage of opportunities to give feed-back, so make sure to create these opportunities. This is a great way for retailers to determine whether they are on the same page with their consumers, in terms of quality and experience.
- Millennials are willing to indulge in the products they believe

are worth indulging in. But, not everyone is going to have the same list of products they are willing to spend on.

- Millennials are willing to pay for quality, so tell them how your products are better than the competition's. Just beware you cannot convince everyone.

CHAPTER 5

ALL-IN-ONE

—

"The millennial generation expects to have the same shopping experience in different sales channels and is driving the convergence of new channels of communication, commerce and service."

— DEBORAH WEINSWIG, MANAGING DIRECTOR
OF FUNG GLOBAL RETAIL & TECHNOLOGY.

"Are you looking for anything specific today?" The sales associate asked Saj, as she walked into a crowded Sephora with her friend.

"I'm looking for a foundation, but, honestly I don't know where to start. I looked online, but there were way too many options to pick from, so I thought I'd come into the store to get more help and actually try on different foundations before buying anything," Saj replied, overwhelmed by even thinking about what she was about to get herself into.

"Yes, I'd be happy to help! Why don't you follow me? I'm going to use our Color IQ technology to help narrow down your choices. Then, we can test your matches and find the best fit for you," the sales associate said, as the three of them walked toward the beauty bar. The associate sat Saj down in front of the large mirror with bright lights.

"Once we get you on our Color IQ system, you can use it in stores, online, and on our app to sort through product and minimize the options you have to pick from when purchasing a product. It's going to come up with a four-digit code, which will automatically be applied to your product searches for the skin and lip categories when you are logged onto your Beauty Insider account."

"Wow, okay, that'll make my life so much easier," Saj joked.

The sales associate got out a weird-looking remote that at first scared Saj a bit. When the associate saw the look on her face, she said, "Don't worry, this is our Color ID device that captures an image of your skin in complete darkness. It allows the tool to focus on your skin's physiology and eliminates variables that can distort shade selection."

Saj didn't really know what any of that meant, but she let the associate go on with what she was doing. She held the device up to three different parts of her skin: both cheeks and her forehead. The device came up with a code that the associate typed it into her iPad.

She went on to ask Saj general questions about her skin, like whether it was oily, and about what she was looking for in her foundation, including how much coverage she wanted, to get a better idea of what direction to go in with all the options she had for a foundation.

The associate put in all the information into the iPad and within a new minutes, she turned to Saj and said, "There you have it! These are the four foundations that are the best match for your skin! Let's go try these on."

"Wow, that was so quick and easy! I would have never been able to narrow it down like this online," Saj said after seeing her options lined up on the screen.

**

When I am shopping for anything, it usually starts online. I'll get an email about a deal that looks promising in the "promotions" tab of my email, and I'll go ahead and open the website's page. This will usually happen while I'm trying to procrastinate on a paper or assignment, so I'll actually take the time to go through all the brand's products. The website is where I first come into contact with the brand and it's offerings. I think of this as the initial "research" stage. If the items are generally standard, like a t-shirt, I'll go ahead and make the purchase online. For other items, which I know from experience I can't buy online, like jeans, shoes, or many beauty products, I'll take the information I get online into the stores, and I'll expect to see the same products, offerings, and promotions in both places. I expect to have the same experience no matter where I am shopping.

I know everyone can relate to not being able to buy jeans online. I buy all my jeans from American Eagle and, from what I've experienced, a size four is not always a size four. That's why buying jeans for me is a big event that I need to plan out in advance. First of all, I'm only going to go to American Eagle to buy jeans if I know they have some that I like, otherwise it's a waste of my time. This is when I check online. After I know I can expect to find something, I'll go ahead and try them on in the physical retail store. I know a lot of online retailers are starting to do free online returns and exchanges, but I'm impatient; when I buy something online, I already have to wait three to five days for shipping and I definitely don't want to wait another week to get the item exchanged if it doesn't fit right the first time. I would much rather go to the store and stand in line to use the fitting room.

There is a common myth about millennials: they are all about technology and online shopping. But that's where marketers are missing the mark.

Yes, it's true that millennials are savvy, online consumers, but that doesn't mean they have stopped stepping foot into brick-and-mortar stores. According to Accenture's Journal of High-Performance Business, when it comes to shopping, 68 percent of all millennials demand an integrated, seamless experience, regardless of the channel. That means being able to transition effortlessly from smartphone to computer to physical store in the quest for the best products and services.

In fact, PwC found that 73 percent of millennials said they still prefer purchasing their products in physical stores, as opposed to online, after browsing on the web.

My friend Mallory can attest to this. She says when shopping online, especially for beauty products, the purchases fall into two categories: favorites and prospects.

When Mallory shops online, mostly at Sephora or MAC, she buys her "favorites" — the products that she uses so frequently that they have become basics in her makeup routine. She told me that foundation, mascara, eyeliner, blush, and bronzer are products she always buys online because she has tried and liked them.

But for "prospective purchases", the internet, especially social media, becomes critical for Mallory's product research. Just imagine scrolling through your Instagram and seeing a beauty blogger promoting a product. Then you head over to Pinterest, where you see that product being promoted again. Next thing you know, you check your email and you have one from the retailer itself. And now with voice recognition, your phone can track your audio searches (thank you Siri) and present you with relevant ads on platforms, like Facebook and Instagram, while you're scrolling through your feed. Simply being reminded of the product will encourage millennials to buy it, since they rely on what they see around them.

In fact, most millennials won't buy something the first time they see it in store. It's all about being reminded of the product multiple times, even through word-of-mouth marketing. Mallory first came to know about the Kat Von D Lip Mats on Sephora's Instagram account. She saw the product and was definitely interested in it, and was persuaded to buy when a friend recommended it to her.

For these consumers, beauty is second nature. They invest time to stay in-the-know to be ahead of the curve. They want to hear about beauty, whether through social media or directly from their friends. They have the power to share the latest news with their networks in a matter of seconds.

That being said, millennials expect a seamless transition between shopping online, on social media, and in stores.

There is a reason why 73 percent of millennials still prefer shopping for beauty products in stores; they have a "try-before-you-buy" mentality. Millennials don't just want to just see a product — they want to test the product to see for themselves if it works. This is the cause for the so-called Sephoraization of the beauty industry.

When I was 16, I was on the hunt for a skin care routine that actually worked for my skin. As I've mentioned, I have very sensitive skin. At the time, it was very oily and I had acne. I had tried dozens of drugstore products but was never able to find one that didn't irritate my skin. It was rejecting everything I put on it and, at that point, I was desperate for any form of miracle.

Before I chose Shiseido's Pureness line for my skin, I was considering Clinique's products, because they claimed to be "dermatologist approved", "allergy tested", and "100 percent fragrance free." My mom had also been using Clinique for years, so that was the first counter she took me to when we walked into Bloomingdales.

The Clinique sales representative asked me about my skin type.

Based on what I told her, she suggested I buy the Clinique Acne-Solutions Foam Cleanser, along with the Clarifying Lotion and All-Over Clearing treatment, which were all in the same line of products.

From my past experiences with using face products, I was very hesitant to buy them right away. I looked at the ingredients on the back of the packaging and saw that the products included a lot of the ones I knew were irritating to my skin.

That's when the sales representative tested the products on my skin. She sat me down and went through all three steps of what my routine would be if I were to buy the products. But after testing out the regime, I realized it was definitely not for me. The products left my skin dry and itchy — the exact opposite of what I wanted.

Unfortunately for Clinique, the sales representative did not get my business that day. But at the Bloomingdales near my home, Clinique shares a counter with Shiseido, and the Shiseido sales representative happened to overhear my concerns. As we were leaving the Clinique counter, she offered to help me try their products. By this time I was desperate, mostly to stop the irritation from the Clinique products I had just tried, so I stopped to learn about the Shiseido products.

She tested all three products from the line she was recommending on me, and I was honestly in disbelief. Finally, there was something that left my skin feeling moisturized but not oily!

I turned to my mom and told her I absolutely had to have this product line, and to this day, it's still the foundation of my every day routine.

If it weren't for actually being able to go into Bloomingdales to try the products, I would have spent $60 on the Clinique line and would have never been able to finish a single bottle.

The "try-before-you-buy" mentality allows these consumers to buy products they know they will like. This is especially critical for retailers, since millennials' price-consciousness means they don't want to have to spend money where they don't in fact need to.

But along with the importance of a good in-store experience, brands can't forget about their presence online.

Millennials are known for making cosmetics purchases online from specialty beauty merchants — 35 percent versus 22 percent — and online sampling programs, such as Birchbox — 23 percent versus 12 percent. They are the technology generation, so of course they are going to use it when they can.

Online shopping is important because millennials have a "finding-the-best-deal" mentality.

Eighty-five percent of 18 to 34-year-olds agreed with the statement that "once I find a product I like, I buy it wherever I can get the best price." It is also much easier and faster to compare the prices of multiple different retailers online than by physically going into the different stores. I'm always trying to find the best deal possible, especially with makeup. Since the products I use the most are the products I have to buy the most, I want to be able to save a few dollars when I can.

There are even websites that offer cash back, like Coupon-Cabin, which I have downloaded onto my laptop. Every time I go on a partnering retailer's website, I get a pop-up at the top of my screen that shows me how much cash back I can get if I make a purchase. Who doesn't want to essentially get paid to shop?

I've also signed up for services like DealCatcher and Retail-MeNot, which send emails with the deals and promotions retailers are offering. Like I said, if I can find a way to save money, I will.

Retailers have to be able to keep up with millennials' online habits and how they are being influenced to make purchases. Retailers know they want to be seen everywhere their consumers are shopping to truly influence their purchasing decisions, both online and in stores. To achieve this, brands have to devise an omni-channel strategy.

Sephora is one retailer that has successfully been able to keep up with millennials' multi-faceted shopping habits by transforming its in-store technology. Julie Bornstein, executive vice president and CMO of the company, explains that "digital is a must for the future of retailing …. We're giving our clients the most customizable experience in the beauty industry, and connecting clients with our experts in the ways that are most relevant to them." Sephora is redefining what it means to shop at physical stores by bridging the online and offline world. Touch-screen devices, for example, which allow consumers to browse through products and read reviews, are making it as easy as possible for customers to find the products they want, in a way that is both familiar and helpful.

Since millennials expect brands to be able to seamlessly integrate all forms of media into their marketing mix, it is essential for retailers to keep up with this growing trend.

Beauty Tips:

- Though millennials are obsessed with social media and technology, brands cannot forget about traditional means of advertising.
- Millennials want a consistent, integrated marketing experience.

They expect their retailers to offer them the same messages and promotions regardless of whether they are shopping online or in-stores, or looking at promotions via email or social media.

- These consumers have a "try-before-you buy" mentality, which is what drives them to brick-and-mortar stores.
- Millennials want to find the best deal out there. Know where they are looking and promote your brands in these places to increase your customer reach.

CHAPTER 6

MODERN MEDIA

"The new celebrities are the social influencers, and quite honestly some make more money than the people who get Emmy Awards."

— JOHN DEMSEY, EXECUTIVE GROUP PRESIDENT
AT ESTÉE LAUDER COSMETICS INC.

"Becca Highlighters are *absolutely* incredible. I've been a big fan of the formula for a really long time. And then, Jaclyn Hill hopped on board and did this insane collaboration, and she just really hit the perfect color for every skin tone," said Tati, also known as GlamourLifeGuru to some, as she sat in front of her camera talking about her "faves and hates" of Becca Cosmetics.

"This is super flattering. This is Champagne Pop, and it did not disappoint," she said while holding the container to the camera as she rubbed some on her finger and swatched it onto the back of her hand.

Nora watched, growing more interested with every word Tati said. "Wow, that does look really nice," she thought to herself.

It was prom season, and Nora had stumbled upon Glamour-LifeGuru when she was searching for prom makeup looks on YouTube. The days before her senior prom were flying by, and she needed to get the perfect look put together for the night. Tati's video about Becca Cosmetics showed up on the side bar of one of the videos she was watching. Nora had never heard of the brand before, so she was curious to see why the video had over 500,000 views.

Once the video ended, Nora opened up a new window and typed "Becca Cosmetics" into the search bar. She clicked on the first link and was taken to the website, where she spent the next hour exploring the pages and looking at all the different products the brand had to offer.

After the amazing comments from Tati and the other products reviews she read online, Nora knew she wanted to use these products for her prom look.

"I remembered hearing about the Becca Highlighter, but I had never actually seen it before. Tati was the first person I ever saw talk about the product. Today, she's the only vlogger I'd ever really trust, who can really convince me to buy a product. She goes really in depth, tests out all the products, makes vlogs where she applies products and checks in throughout the day with updates about how they are holding up. She tries every product she's reviewing, which tells me she really knows what she's talking about."

**

The first time I heard about Urban Decay's Naked Palette, when it came out a few years ago, was while watching a "get-ready-with-me" tutorial on YouTube. I immediately paused the video to go to the Urban Decay website to check out the palette. I was never really one to use eyeshadow that much, because I didn't like the bold colors that I always saw being used together. However, I was interested in the Naked Palette because of it's natural and subtle colors. The video I was watching also suggested which colors to use together and gave tips on how to best apply the product. Judging by the vlogger's love for the palette, it became something that I constantly thought about buying. After I saw it being reviewed by dozens of other bloggers, I went out and bought it for myself.

I'm sure you have heard of Arielle Charnas, Alexis Ren, Zoella, or Lauren Conrad (my personal favorite blogger). They have become the new "it" influencers by posting, snapping, tweeting, and sharing to their hundreds of thousands, even millions, of followers, who then rush out to buy the products they recommend.

Take Arielle Charnas, of Something Navy, for instance. Last year, she posted about the Peter Thomas Roth Rose Stem Cell Bio-Repair Gel Mask on her Snapchat story. Then, within 24 hours of posting her story, there were 502 masks sold, or $17,565 worth of product. At the same rate, it works out to be $123,000 in sales in a week, $527,000 in a month, and almost $6.4 million in a year.

You might just think it was a coincidence, but when she snapped about Yves Saint Laurent's Mascara Volume Effet Faux Cils Shocking in Deep Black, it led to the sale of 422 units in 24 hours of her post, driving $13,500 in sales. Once again, $95,000 worth of mascara in a week, $405,000 in a month, and $4.9 million in a year.

This is something worth using to your advantage.

In the past, bloggers were seen as "pretend journalists" who took the roles of beauty editors. But millennials view them as something different. According to Forbes, 33 percent of millennials rely mostly on blogs before they make a purchase. They look at social media as an authentic lens to view the world with, placing more and more trust on their favorite social media influencers.

Data collected by TubularInsights reports that 60 percent of millennials would try a product suggested by a YouTuber, and 33 percent consider blogs to be a top media source when researching a purchase.

To millennials, bloggers and digital influencers have credibility. I know I can say that the bloggers I follow are those whom I trust to receive advice and tips from. I know they are being honest about their opinions and feedback, and they are able to connect with me at a deeper level than traditional ads blasted by marketers. Millennials don't view traditional advertisements as genuine and personal, since they are skeptical and weary of marketers' intentions to persuade them to buy the products brands are trying to sell — which I'll return to in Chapter 7.

Additionally, I'm simply more likely to consider products bloggers use and recommend — or don't — because I know they have had a positive — or negative — experience with them, otherwise, they wouldn't advocate for it. Ninety-two percent of consumers rely on referrals from people they know over anything else when making purchases, and for millennials, the authenticity of YouTubers can make their recommendations feel like they are coming from a friend.

If I'm scrolling through my Instagram feed and I see a blogger featuring a product, I tend to click on the tag before I can even decide if I am interested in the product or not. I simply want to get more information about where this person is shopping and what they are buying, partially because I know that since I follow them, I have a reason to like the product. From there, I will usually check out the retailer's individual Instagram page, and, if I am interested in what it has to offer, I will click on the website link and look through all its products. This usually starts off as a five-minute break from whatever I'm doing, but it can turn into a twenty-minute process and another way for me to procrastinate.

This happens to me all the time. For the past couple of years, I have had trouble falling asleep and sleeping through the night. I follow Sarah's Day on every form of social media out there: Facebook, Instagram, Snapchat, YouTube — you name it. Sarah is a health and fitness blogger and vlogger from Australia, who shares her stories about her daily life, what she eats, her workouts, and anything else she wants to share with her followers. I follow her because she's a genuine and down-to-earth person, so she is always honest and open about everything she does.

In the first clip of one of her Instagram stories, Sarah started off by talking about how she has had trouble sleeping ever since she was a young kid. This lured me in. She talked about how even her dad has trouble sleeping, and how she has tried everything possible to find a way to sleep through the night. She said, since she really believes in the power of scent therapy, one product she has been using is Flora Remedia's Rose Geranium Flower Calming Treatment Oil for her stress and anxiety. She described how she heard about the brand's Lavender Sleep Treatment Oil and just got her a bottle in the mail. She told her followers that she was excited to try it and would tell everyone what her review was the next day.

Knowing I also had similar sleep problems, though maybe not as extreme as hers, I went straight to Flora Remedia's website to look at the products. Sarah even had a discount code. I would have bought the product right then and there, but I'm still waiting to see what she has to say about it. If it works, I'm going to order it right away.

But the point is that she got me to their website. She did exactly what the brand wanted, in a way that allowed her to genuinely and authentically connect with consumers.

In her article, *Instagram: Shopping Venue For Beauty?* Jennifer Sain talks about how Instagram is starting to "break the barrier between exploration and purchase in the social media space."

She notes that the beauty company Glossier was "reportedly one of the first brands, and the only beauty brand, to beta test

Instagram's shopping feature. The feature allows users to tap photos to view products and prices. Once a user taps on a product, he or she is directed to a landing page where he or she can complete a purchase. L2 Inc. writes that while Instagram shopping is not yet available to all brands, beauty brands may be able to leverage the social shopping platform, particularly for impulse and social purchasing."

"All of that said," Sain goes on to write, "there is a reason beauty marketers are cautious about selling on Instagram. Twitter recently removed its buy button, as did Facebook. And analysts say Instagram and Pinterest are struggling. Digiday says that buy buttons have struggled on social platforms because 'transactions have been clunky, inventory has been mismanaged and consumer intent was never properly understood.' "

"Users don't currently buy on social networks," says Jessica Lui, social marketing senior analyst at Forrester. "Users are much more likely to discover and explore brands, products and services on social media than they are to buy."

But for more brands to begin successfully integrating buy features, or to simply continue increasing product awareness on social media, it is crucial for them know who their consumers are and know where they are shopping.

There are many brands that, though they do manage to sell to millennials, are still dependent on advertising through traditional channels, like magazines and television. For instance, Clinique's average consumers starts at age 45 and are traditional shoppers who buy products in stores and who like receiving bonus gifts with purchases. That's why not every brand can jump on the bandwagon.

And needless to say, traditional advertising is a medium that should *never* be overlooked. It is an easy way to remind consumers of the brands and continue making them aware of the offerings, whether it be while flipping through a magazine or driving down the street.

But now think about Estée Lauder. For years, the company relied heavily on traditional advertising, but then, realized traditional methods were ineffective at reaching millennials, who were starting to make up a significant portion of its consumer base. In response, the company re-allocated its marketing budget, putting its largest portion towards its digital strategy, which ranged from paid search to content, and influencers.

In 2014, the company used a portion its new digital budget to partner with social media influencers, including Kendall Jenner. Today, she has over 78.3 million followers on Instagram, one of which I am proud to be. However, followers does not equate to guaranteed success. Needless to say this partnership was a huge risk; Estée Lauder would be using a girl who was 19 at the time, while the brand is targeted to women over twice her age.

Luckily, the collaboration paid off. Estée Lauder has the fourth largest e-commerce presence among Beauty brands in the United States, the UK, France, and China combined — after Bobbi Brown, Clarins and Clinique. And Estée Lauder is not the only brand within the company to be shifting its focus to digital; Lancôme and Mackler are also starting to see the importance of bloggers.

Experience is what millennials are looking for. They want something they can relate to, something that speaks to them personally, something that they know to be true. For beauty companies, the goal of partnering with influencers is for them to share their experience with the brand and with the products. Followers want to see through the lens of other consumers and feel like they have authentic exposure to their lives, hoping to have similar experiences if they, too, purchase those products.

Mallory agrees: "With makeup, I think a large part of the experience is being able to try, see, and interact with the products, in addition to sales helps. I tend to only order products online if I already know I like them or have at least tried them before. I like to turn to bloggers to see what they have to say about their experience with a product if I can't physically get my hands on it before making a purchase. Even if I can go in stores to try the product, I'll use bloggers as a way to see if it is even worth the trip to the store. Getting to see what their experience was with the product gives me a good sense of what I can expect my experience to be like."

It's important to realize that influencers are no longer only bloggers. Instead, they are regular people who share much, if not most, of their lives, through YouTube, Twitter, Instagram, Snapchat, or all of these platforms.

Today, Snapchat is one of the most popular social medial platforms, becoming the most powerful vehicle for influencers to connect with their followers. It has now become ingrained in me to always open my Snapchat app when I first unlock my phone. I'm embarrassed to say it, but I could probably get to the app with my eyes closed.

Arielle Charnas explains, "We're [bloggers] pretty much documenting everything and every move — I don't think any editor or journalist puts everything out there like we do. It's definitely completely different; I don't know if it's something you can define [yet]."

Bloggers are no longer seen only on social platforms, but are also expanding their presence on different channels.

"Blogger engagement used to happen only in the digital world, but now it inspires a full integrated communication plan, which can be leveraged on the consistency of a genuine story. That's the upcoming way of doing marketing," said Alessio Sanzogni, group general manager of Chiara Ferragni, Theblondesalad.com, and Chiara Ferragni Collection.

And these partnerships are a two-way street: brands want bloggers and bloggers want brands. Brands want to see a rise in their social media followings to increase brand awareness and recall, while social media stars want to build their audience.

But digital influences aren't all paid. You don't need to have millions of followers to influence others. Even you and I could do it.

Millennials are influenced by those they interact with and relate to the most, whether in person or through social media. They look to friends and family to help them in their decision-making process.

I know I always ask my friends for their opinion before I buy something, since I want to make sure that what I'm buying is actually worth it and that others will approve of it. I also tend to look at blogs and reviews to get opinions from other influencers I relate to.

It's clear to see that in today's day and age, a digital presence is inevitable. The challenge becomes how to manage it.

Beauty Tips:

- Millennials are present all over social media, so they expect you to be present on all the same platforms.
- Increase your social media presence by partnering with bloggers to promote and speak about your products. Millennials trust these personas more than traditional advertising.
- Millennials want to know what they are buying before they actually make a purchase. They turn to blogs and reviews for more information about products from people they know they can trust to be honest.
- Millennials trust brands they can relate to. No matter who it is, they want the opinions of others to confirm their decisions.

CHAPTER 7

NEW SPEECH

———

"The future of advertising is not advertising."

— REBECCA KANTAR, FOUNDER OF IMBELLUS,
A TECHNOLOGY COMPANY THAT IS REINVENTING
HOW WE MEASURE HUMAN POTENTIAL.

"Welcome to the new world of Proactive," Julianne Hough exclaimed enthusiastically.

Saj looked up from her book to see Julianne on her TV screen, while she sat on the couch doing homework after school.

"Hmm this could be useful," Saj said to herself, turning her attention away from her work.

"I'm Julianne Hough, and if you're anything like me, your skin is not always clear," Julianne said, as though she was speaking directly to Saj. "If acne is keeping you out of the picture, it's time to do something about it."

As a 13-year-old middle-schooler starting to get acne, Saj wanted to find a quick solution.

"Introducing the New Proactive," the voice of a man said, as the products centered the TV screen, "now faster and gentler than ever before."

Before-and-after pictures started to appear on the screen, trying to prove to Saj that the products were truly effective. "I really love the New Proactive," one user said on screen. The ad then went on to talk about the science behind the micro-crystal medicines that "deliver instant acne-fighting action."

Everything was telling Saj to try the products, but she was skeptical.

Like many millennials today, Saj was never really swayed by ads because she felt they were biased. "I personally don't really believe in them, especially if they are trying to sell me something," she told me, as she turned her head away from the TV to face me at the other end of the couch.

She stands by that today, saying, "I feel like if you try too hard to advertise and push your products, they must not be good because you are trying to overcompensate for the products through excessive advertising."

**

The last time I actively watched a commercial was during the Superbowl. Besides that, I can't recall the last time I sat down on the couch to leisurely watch TV. I prefer watching shows on Netflix, everyone's beloved, ad-free streaming site.

Gone are the days of watching TV or reading magazines. Millennials are on entirely new platforms and devices, doing everything through technology.

This has become a prime location for retailers to place their advertising content.

But even traditional ads are not resonating with millennials, regardless of where they are placed.

According to Matthew Tyson from Huffington Post, only 1 percent of millennials say that a compelling ad influences them and would make a brand more trustworthy. They don't want to be blasted with irrelevant information. If ads don't mean anything to millennials, it doesn't matter what the retailer is selling — they won't be influenced by them.

Millennials value authenticity and honesty. They know retailers are purposefully creating ads to try to get consumers to buy their products, and therefore, don't see them as truthful. They find ways to skip commercials and avoid ads that pop up on social media. They simply are not influenced by advertising the same way their parents were.

**

Monday night, Neha was watching "The Bachelor" online with her roommates, since they didn't have cable in their apartment. They sat on the couch with a laptop in the middle of their coffee table and glasses of wine in their hands.

"Why aren't you guys watching the commercials?" Neha asked about half-way through the show. When she looked over to her roommates, she noticed that every time the show cut to a commercial break, they would all first freak out over what just happened, taking their best guesses for who was not going to get the final rose, then immediately pull out their phones and open Instagram or Snapchat to see whatthey missed in the 10 minutes since the last commercial.

"The reason I'm watching the show in the first place is to watch the show. If I can be doing other things when it's not on, I'm going to do that. I just don't find the ads important or relevant to me, so I don't really pay attention," said Tessa, looking up from her phone.

⁜

I will admit that online commercials are even more frustrating to sit through than that ones on TV, so it makes sense why they weren't watching them. But I can't say I share the same habits. I'm interested in commercials to see what marketers are doing to reach out to consumers.

But Tessa has a point that many millennials will agree on: why waste time on something that doesn't mean anything to them?

That's why advertisers have to find a way for consumer to connect and create an emotional attachment with the brand. They need to feature the content, the product, and an experience, allowing them speak to millennials in a way that will make them want to listen. This requires brands to approach their consumers in a new way — one that focuses on authenticity and value, rather than sales.

One way to start is by making millennials like the brand. This doesn't mean to make them like the products, but rather the story, the value, and the relationship the brand is selling. This will help the brand build trust with their consumers.

And what better way to do this than through engagement?

These consumers want something real. They crave interaction.

Forbes found that 62 percent of millennials are more likely to become loyal fans if a brand engages them on social networks. They expect brands not only to be present on social networks, but to engage with them while they are there.

Just like in any other relationships, millennials want transparency — they need to know you before they can trust you. They want brands to interact with them so they can be assured they are interacting with human beings, not faceless retailers who just want their money.

But how did this distrust even originate?

Well, we can thank the internet and social media for that. Millennials know information is instantaneously available. Everyone is connected, and everyone is capable of searching anything online. As a result, millennials don't want to have look for the truth. They would rather have brands be honest. They want authentic messages and interactions, not over-the-top ads, big promises, and insane wows factor.

What does this mean to marketers and retailers?

They need to rethink their strategy to reach consumers.

Think of Neutrogena ads: they're very clean, minimalistic, straight to the point, and honest. You'll see Hayden Panettiere, Kristen Bell, Kerry Washington, and most recently, Olivia Holt, star in the ads. And the one thing that most of these ads try to assure the viewer is that the products actually work.

The one Neutrogena commercial that I see all the time is for the Makeup Remover Cleansing Towelettes. "Does your makeup remover take it all off? Neutrogena makeup remover does." And then we see Kerry Washington use the wipe to show that the makeup remover actually works.

That is exactly what millennials want: to know that the product is able to live up to its claims.

When talking about ads Theresa said, "When it comes to makeup, I am more product-focused, meaning I am more inclined to like the brand and the product if they are presented to me in a way that features how they are used in a utilitarian way. It is more impactful for me to see how mascara looks as a swatch, rather than already applied on a model. That way, I have a better sense of what I can expect if I do choose to buy it."

Another method of creating meaningful and powerful ads is by taking advantage of user-generated content, which is easier than ever to get a hold of with the rise of social media and online communities.

Not only do millennials trust user-generated content 50 percent more than any other media, but they find it 35 percent more memorable than non-user-generated content and traditional media.

What better way to present consumers with the content they want than by having them create it themselves?

When it comes to reaching millennials, they themselves are the most valuable resources a brand can use.

It all ties back to trust. This generation wants social proof — to see that brands are actually delivering where they said they would. Showing consumers your products in action can be all it takes to convince them to make a purchase.

By contrast, trying to tell millennials your brand is better than others is less impactful. It is much more powerful to let them see the product or service through the eyes of other customers. Seventy-six percent of consumers view content created by an average person as more honest than the ads created by the brands themselves.

User-generated content is essentially free marketing. Why

wouldn't you take advantage of it?

Sephora did. The company created the Beauty Board featured on its website that curates consumers' photos from social media and shows off the products they are wearing in the pictures. From the Beauty Board, consumers can see exactly what a product looks like once it has been used. It makes it easier to explore different products and shades, and even match skin tones with products. This is especially useful for online beauty shopping, since it is hard to determine what a product will look like once applied, without having tried it before hand. By giving consumers a point of reference, Sephora is using user-generated content to put forth genuine advocacies for its products.

Another successful example of user-generated content is MAC's "MACnificent Me" campaign. MAC created a whole experience for its consumers, who submitted their content in the form of a mantra that "illustrated their style, heart, and soul," along with a 100-word essay, and photo, from which they chose winners to get make overs. MAC wanted to find their winner based on messages of positivity and empowerment, rather than pictures of each contestant.

Users could personalize the color, font, and design of their submissions and look at what other contestants said. The site encouraged engagement and allowed participants to feel connected and invested in the campaign.

MAC's campaign received a total of 100,000 mantras and increased traffic on its website and social media. Visitors spent over eight minutes on the site looking at other mantras and engaging with the brand.

For brands, of course, there's a huge advantage to using this type of free marketing.

I personally love ads that show real people, because it tells me the brands are not trying to hide anything or trick me into buying their product or service. I'm able to trust them more and it's this trust that will help them develop loyal and lasting relationships with their consumers.

Beauty Tips:

- Millennials want more than a faceless brand. They want a personal relationship that adds value to their life, so traditional advertising is not as meaningful to them anymore.
- Millennials are sold by stories, relationships, experiences, and value, not by bland facts.
- Millennials want to be a part of user-generated content. It makes them feel like their voice means something to the brand. It's a great way to get free advertising for your brand, while also showing your consumers you care about them.

CHAPTER 8

PERSONALIZED CONCENTRATE

———

"Be relevant."

— JOE CAVALIER, CHIEF CUSTOMER
OFFICER AT NEWELL-RUBBERMAID.

"To celebrate my birthday," blogger Bella Gerard said, "I headed to New York with my mom and sister to create some personalized lipsticks at the Bit Lip Lab in SoHo. I'd read about it online, and we thought it would be the perfect way to combine our two favorite things: celebrations and makeup."

"All three of us decided to try out the Bespoke Lipstick option, which allows you to create two custom lip colors with the help of your lip lab artist."

"After explaining to our artists the types of shades we were looking for, they mixed up a ton of options for us to test out. Once we exfoliated, masked, and prepped our lips, we were able to try them on and make adjustments to our liking."

"The artists were super patient with us throughout the process; we are three picky girls, especially when it comes to our makeup, and we wanted to make sure we got what we paid for. I ended up selecting a pinky nude and a more warm-toned brown nude, the latter of which looks a lot like my very favorite liquid lipstick, Kylie's Exposed."

"After perfecting our shades, we got to name the colors and choose our finish. I went with mostly creamy, sheer finishes, while my sister, Morgan, opted for mattes. We then got to choose the scent for each of our lipsticks — I gave both of mine a minty vanilla smell that I'm totally obsessed with."

"Next the shades were mixed and poured, and then the bullets were packaged in Bite's signature lipstick tubes."

"Overall, the experience took just about an hour for the three of us. The price tag was major — $150 for two lipsticks — but they did package the lippies in super cute Bite boxes and bags, and included for each of us a cherry lip scrub, an agave lip mask, and a Bite lip primer."

"If you're a perfectionist and a makeup junkie, Bite Lip Lab is your dream — it's practically designed for picky people, as you get to ensure the color you purchase is completely perfect, from the shade right down to the finish and scent."

**

Not only is the millennial generation the largest in the United States, but it is also the most racially diverse. Millennials are all unique. They have different wants, needs, interests, goals, aspirations, and desires. As a result, each individual in this generation expects to be treated as exactly that: an individual.

I'll admit it, the first time I saw a personalized ad on my laptop, I was terrified. Only a couple hours before it showed up on a random news article I was reading online, I was looking at shoes on Steve Madden's website. (I think it's safe to say that I have an online shopping addiction.) After being on that website, banner ads were popping up everywhere while I was on other sites, with the exact shoes that I was looking at! I was amazed at how that was even possible, but, also concerned that someone was tracking everything I was doing on the internet. Not that I have anything to hide, but it was still a little creepy.

After a while, I got used to it and actually liked having those little reminders and suggestions show up here and there. It tells me that brands are paying attention to what I like. I know that even if the girl sitting next to me in class was also looking at Steve Madden's website, the banner ads that would show up on her screen would definitely not be the same as mine. Mine would be personal and specific for me, based on what products I was looking at on the website.

Brands can't rely on traditional segmentation, done on a geographical and demographical bases, such as sex, age, income, and location. For example, let's look at the segment females between the ages of 18-34 who have a mid-range income living in Washington, D.C. There is a clear problem: it's not specific enough to rely on. It's simply too broad to allow a brand to focus on its core, target consumer. What about occupation, hobbies, and lifestyle? Brands need to re-think their segmentation and position themselves to connect with their specific consumers.

Instead, try phrasing it towards the women who are constantly on the go with less than 15 minutes to get ready in the morning. They are looking for a one-step, all-in-one primer, concealer, and foundation customized to match their skin to make them feel effortlessly flawless and ready to take on their busy lives. That's way more specific than anyone's typical demographics.

It becomes important to be able to target your consumers and speak to them in a way that makes them know you're specifically reaching out to them. This will allow you to appear more relevant in the minds of consumers, because they will know that *your* brand, not another one, can speak to their individual needs.

This is where personalization — engagement at the right time with the right content — becomes important.

Personalization can be done in a dozens of different ways, from writing very targeted blog posts for specific types of interests, such as food, fitness, beauty, and travel, to engaging in one-to-one social media conversions with consumers. I'm sure you've seen the article: "Wendy's Is Roasting People On Twitter, And It's Just Too Funny." Even the fast food joint is directly responding to consumers and creating one-to-one interactions with them.

That's why two-way communication on social media is a must. It's the easiest way to create personalized interactions with consumers and show them they are valued by the brand. And this goes beyond simply responding to tweets and liking comments: engaging with consumers means adding value to their experience. This can be done through loyalty programs, recognition events, and special access to sales and other promotional events. Econsultancy reports that businesses personalizing web experiences on average see a 19 percent increase in sales.

With these strategies, brands are able to connect with millennials at a deeper level, making them feel as though their needs are being prioritized and that marketers are connecting with their specific niche, whether they are foodies or beauty gurus. But one size does not fit all. One message will not affect different consumers the same way. Brands have to realize they are reaching out to a diverse group of consumers, which means a diverse range in taste in goods and differences in how each individual want to be marketed to.

In the beauty industry, personalization can take two meanings: personalized products and personalized marketing.

At the product level, brands including Lancôme, Khiel's, and MAC, offer custom products that can be tailored to their individual needs. A beauty adviser at Lancôme will scan my skin tone to blend together a one-of-a-kind Le Teint Particulier Custom Foundation. She will then put it in a personalized bottle with a "Complexion ID" signifying my individual blend, so I can recreate it when I run out. If you ask me, that's pretty amazing. No more swatching on my hand and neck, or struggling to find the perfect shade that may be too light or dark for my skin. MAC has found a simple solution to another problem many of us can relate to: only using one or two colors on an eyeshadow palette. The retailer gives me   the option to make my own palette, where I can pick and choose the colors I want to have, all together on a palette of two, four, fifteen, or thirty. It makes carrying makeup easier and more convenient by putting my favorite eyeshadows on a compact and portable palette.

But personalization doesn't end there. These beauty brands, along with many others, are giving their consumers personalized product suggestions offered by beauty apps or targeted marketing messages through social media platforms, like Instagram and Snapchat, or even on the internet through banner ads.

The benefit of looking at personalized marketing is that it can be done anywhere: online, in store, and on social media. You name it, and a brand has probably already done it.

Millennials not only want, but expect, a personalized experience that results from retailers knowing their preferences and interests. In fact, a recent Infosys survey reported that 78 percent of consumers are more likely to become repeat customers if a retailer provides them with targeted and personalized offers. Not doing so can actually be detrimental; over half of U.S. and Canadian consumers have said they considered not returning to retailers who don't give them tailored and relevant offers.

Amazon does a great job of presenting its consumers with personalized information and offers through its "More Picks

For You," "Consumers Who Bought This Item Also Bought," and "Your Recommendations" sections on its website.

For example, by clicking on the "Your Recommendations" link, consumers are taken to a page filled with products recommended specifically for that user. The recommendations are based on categories that the consumer has previously viewed and presents them with a range of products from all those different areas. The goal is to present the consumer with products that they are most likely to click on and learn more about, with the hopes of getting another sale. I personally always scroll through those options and will click on the products to get more information about them.

Amazon's recommendation algorithm is a great way to create a personalized online shopping experience, which helps companies increase the average value of orders and the total revenue generated from each customer.

This is a system that many more companies are picking up, including beauty retailers like NARS and Sephora.

"I love the personalized ads that show up on my browser! That's how I've found some of my best purchases. I was even able to find my dress for senior ball using those, so I definitely think they're super helpful," said my friend Yasmeen.

There are clearly many ways to create meaningful and purposeful personalized experiences online, but it becomes slightly harder when consumers are shopping in stores. Millennials go to physical retail stores for the experience more than anything else. They don't necessarily need to make the trip to the store to purchase a product if they can find everything they need online.

With the ease that comes with online shopping, and the individualized experience that can be created on the internet, retailers need to find new and innovative ways to create personalized experiences in stores. This can be slightly more challenging, but brands have found fun and creative ways to do so.

Brands, including Estée Lauder and L'Oréal, have expanded their basis of personalization and have successfully created features on their website, app, and in stores that allow users to upload a picture of themselves or stand in front of a camera to see what products look like on them before buying.

I know a lot of people who love to go into a beauty store or counter and have the beautician help them with everything. Even though I like to shop on my own without any help, I appreciate having a sales associate who is available, knowledgeable, and helpful when I have a question or want advice. I usually expect a high level of service from makeup stores and counters since experience is gaining importance in all retail settings. In beauty, a large part of the experience is being able to try the product, in addition to getting sales help. Trying on products is a unique and personalized experience the retailer is creating for me. For example, associates at Sephora ask what you're looking for, what type of skin you have, and other similar questions, to try to get the perfect product in your hands. They take care of one customer at a time and personalize the experience for them.

So, there you have it. Retailers are pushing personalization by sending customized emails, tailoring deals based on previous purchase behavior, creating a "recommended products" section, and even changing in-store experience. Personalization promotes happy consumers and more importantly, loyal consumers. Therefore, brands need to keep learning about who is buying their products and personalizing the advertising content to stay relevant in the minds of consumers.

Beauty Tips:

- Millennials are all very unique, so make sure you know exactly who your brand is targeting and align your missions and values with the qualities your consumers seek.
- Personalization is key to connecting with millennials at a deeper and more meaningful level. Allow them to personalize

their experience and present them with individualized options, whether it be in-stores or online.

- Millennials want personalized experiences no matter where they are shopping. They want brands to create a customized shopping experience tailored to their individual preferences.

CHAPTER 9

UP THE AMP

"Millennials don't just want to buy your brand, they want to be a part of it. They're looking for ways to participate."

— JEFF FROMM, EXECUTIVE VICE PRESIDENT OF BARKLEY

& CO-AUTHOR OF "MARKETING TO MILLENNIALS".

"How can we capture the minds of millennials?" Rachel Martino, assistant manager of global social media at Origins, asked herself. She was sitting at the head of a conference table, looking out the window with a view of Central Park on a sunny Monday morning as she waited for everyone to gather into the room.

Origins already has a strong following among women in their 30s and 40s, but it wanted to get more millennials on board. Who wouldn't? It's an 80-million-strong demographic who is spending $1 trillion a year.

"We [want] to see what [will] resonate with a 25-year-old woman, since we are looking to her as our next consumer," 24-year-old Rachel said as she turned to her team. "We [want] to catch her at a time in her life when we could really speak to her and draw her into the brand."

But Rachel knew that trying to target a new market was no small task. She was ready to dive into research to produce new products, marketing campaigns, and even a new brand design.

Origins' leadership knew that the most effective and meaningful way to gain this insight was through co-creation, a popular buzzword passed around a lot among management that encompasses bringing consumers into every stage of the business process.

"The idea is not just to create products for a particular kind of consumer, but *with* that consumer. We are going to set up workshops in the United States and China, inviting hundreds of 20-year-olds to discuss their lifestyles, dreams, needs, and desires — and not just as they relate to skincare."

But Rachel knew that having the right product would only be part of the solution. What was equally important was for Origins to be able to speak the language of millennials before actually marketing its products to them.

"Before reaching out to our consumers," she said, "we need to tap into the minds of our millennial employees, which is why we are all seated here today. Brands don't often use their youngest employees in smart ways."

As the meeting went on, "the term 'quarter-life crisis' kept coming up as a playful way to describe 20-year-olds' sense of being constantly in flux between childhood and adulthood. And the idea also had wider cultural traction: the hashtag #QuarterLifeCrisis regularly pops up on Twitter, Facebook, and Instagram connected with funny portraits of everyday life as a millennial."

"The team felt the phrase would be the perfect motto for the new Original Skin serum, since it was specific enough to resonate with millennials, but also broad enough so that everyone would have a personal take on it."

"People in our generation expect to engage in a one-to-one dialogue with brands," Rachel said. "Social media is a great way to engage with 20-year-olds who may not be visiting stores, since they live their lives online."

Rachel and her team decided that the best way to do this was by posting on social media about what it's like to be a 20-year-old:

"When life gets real and you miss college"; "When you make plans to go out, but you really want to stay in, stream videos, and eat takeout"; "Marry him, or break up? Maybe travel the world, find a hot Spaniard, and live on the coast of Ibiza." This became Origins' hundred-percent digital "quarter-life crisis" campaign, sharing news about the serum on social media and through a wide network of bloggers and YouTube influencers."

"Millennials are looking for brands that get them, beyond just what their products can do," Rachel explained to her team. "This approach [is] more about creating a millennial lifestyle and a place where they can talk about all the things that are going on in their lives. We are inserting ourselves into an existing conversation, rather than creating our own, which would be more authentic."

Rachel dismissed the meeting and put her team to work. Then, after the initial research was done, the final area of concern for Rachel was making sure that the campaign design was perfectly aligned with the sensibilities of millennials, which is not an easy task, since aesthetics are very subjective.

Rachel and her team found that the "co-creating workshops yielded one valuable piece of information: [20-year-olds] spend a lot of time on the internet, surrounded with computer-generated fonts and graphics, so the images that stand out to them are often not digital, but hand-drawn. Millennials are more likely to notice calligraphy or illustrated images."

And the imagery for the Origins "quarter-life campaign" came about simply by chance. Mark Ferdman, a VP at Origins who just so happened to enjoy drawing in his spare time, noticed the work of a 25-year-old artist from Nova Scotia, Bee Stanton, on his Instagram feed. Ferdman thought Stanton would be a great fit to create the look of the campaign.

"After taking my doodles to groups of [20-year-olds] to see their reactions, he offered me the whole campaign," said Stanton. "I was over the moon. I was absolutely beside myself."

This is typically not how brands secure artwork for large-scale, big-budget campaigns, however, originality is why millennials resonated and gravitated to the doodles. They felt personal, rather than like the work of large corporations.

"We've been submerged in the online world right from the start," Stanton tells me. "There are so many images competing for our attention, so we have a finely tuned sense of when things are different or authentic. Origins seems to get that about millennials."

After days and nights of hard work, Rachel sat at her desk and looked at the statistics. After only a couple of months, the #QuarterLifeCrisis app had been downloaded by more than 5,000 consumers worldwide. And that was only the start of the new journey.

**

Millennials are doers, participators, and creators.

Co-creation is the fastest and most efficient way for a brand to meet consumer demand and identify more opportunities for growth within the company and beyond. Co-creation is defined as an "active, creative, and social process, based on collaboration between producers and users, that is initiated by the firm to generate value for consumers." It's an outside-in approach where brands focus on their users to allow companies and consumers to create joint value at multiple points of interaction, which has allowed for innovation and a better customer experience.

By giving most of its power to consumers, co-creating contrasts greatly from open innovation, which is when a firm's internal and external knowledge and technologies are respectively used to accelerate internal innovations and expand the market for external use of innovation.

Frito-Lay used co-creation in its marketing strategy a few years ago. Its Facebook campaign, #DoUsAFlavor, gave its consumers the opportunity to create their own chip flavor with the chance to win a million dollars and have the flavor become a reality.

I jumped into this contest right away — partly because of the money I could win, since, as I mentioned, millennials are price-conscious and always looking for a great deal. Though I knew the chances of actually winning were slim, I still wanted to try to create a product that could potentially resonate with thousands of other people. I was ecstatic my ideas could influence the company's product creations.

The flavor I suggested was cinnamon raisin, which I personally think wasn't too far off from the flavor that won: the chicken and waffles flavor. Just like cinnamon raisin, chicken and waffles incorporated a sweet twist on a classic savory snack.

Lay's was so successful with its campaign that the company took it all around the world. Ranging from Canada, all the way to India, Lay's has been able to interact with its consumers to create fun and new flavors, for, and by, consumers.

After all, a brand's consumers are the ones who will be purchasing the products, so it makes sense to look directly for their input. A contest is a great incentive to get consumers excited and invested in the brand, while also generating more buzz about it!

This all ties back in with feedback. This generation is more than willing to provide brands with feedback, since it means a better product and user experience for themselves.

Millennials want to interact with brands, to co-create products, and to participate in the brand experience. They want their voices to be heard.

Today, an increasing number of brands are giving consumers a bigger role in the creation and development of their products.

When I asked Meg about her experience participating in the #DoUsAFlavor campaign, she said, "I love the fact that companies are reaching out to me and are encouraging me to tell them what I want. It shows me that they are taking the extra steps to create products that actually suit me. Being a part of the process allows me to have input and a voice behind what companies are doing."

"I had a lot of free time over winter break," she continued, making fun of herself. "I made two entries. The first one was butter chicken-flavored chips, which is essentially just like french fries covered in curry sauce — I mean, who wouldn't like that? And the second one was a puffy textured chip. It turned out they already had a puffy chip, so I got disqualified, but it was still pretty exciting being a part of the whole process."

It's clear that brands are increasing interaction with their consumers to create a more meaningful and involved experience, making them appear more approachable and reachable than ever before.

Brands want to please their consumers by creating new and innovative products to constantly keep them engaged with their company. Every brand's ultimate goal is to grow and make money.

This is exactly what cosmetic companies are doing, too.

Brands are reaching out to their consumers through every channel possible, especially social media, since it's the easiest and most direct way to reach their target market.

According to a recent report issued by Ipsos Open Thinking Exchange, the average person spends nearly two hours, approximately 116 minutes, on social media every day, which translates to a total of five years and four months spent over an average lifetime.

When it's broken down, the time spent on social media varies across each platform. YouTube comes in first, consuming over 40 minutes of a person's day, for a total of one year and 10 months in a lifetime. Facebook users spend an average of 35 minutes a day, totaling one year and seven months in a lifetime. Snapchat and Instagram are next with 25 minutes and 15 minutes spent per day, respectively. And, finally, users spend about one minute on Twitter, which is the same as 18 days of usage in a lifetime.

On top of that, Ipsos Open Thinking Exchange data from 2013 shows that some millennials spend more than 3.6 hours per day on social media sites. In addition to gathering feedback on existing products, social media engagement presents an opportunity to obtain insights into what beauty and cosmetics users want. Approaching consumers and speaking directly with them allows brands to create products that address their real — not just assumed — beauty concerns by using methods that are shifting away from traditional research and development.

Nivea co-developed a black and white deodorant with its consumers by relying on two co-creation tactics: netnography, a method of gaining consumer insight from social media, and online co-creation, which was used to further develop and enrich those ideas.

Netnography uses ethnographic research methods to allow companies to look at their consumers' online conversations to understand the emotional, social, and cultural context behind their product experiences. It focuses on listening to consumers, rather than asking them, and understanding their attitudes and behavior, rather than measuring them.

Nivea realized its consumers were a valuable source of information, and started by using netnography as a way to enter into its consumer's world before integrating the consumer's voice. Nivea wanted to gain authentic insights on needs, wishes, concerns, consumer language, and potential product solutions, which it found both implicitly and explicitly posed online and on social media. From there, the company was able to identify three common topics most talked about by its consumers: type of stains, cause of stains, and stain removal.

This step allowed Nivea to take advantage of online co-creation, which give consumers the opportunity generate, enrich, and evaluate ideas and concepts. Co-creation uses integrated communication, such as online discussion boards, that allow for both user-to-user and user-to-company free-flowing interaction.

Through this method, the brand presented consumers with deodorant ideas verbally and visually, and allowed them to use drag-and-drop tools to create lists of their ideal products. By incorporating the voice of consumers, Nivea was able to find the best solutions to these topics.

After evaluating the feedback received from both its methods of co-creation, Nivea created its Black & White deodorant that addressed two of its consumers' biggest concerns: preventing white staining on black and preventing yellow staining on white. The product provided users with 48-hour protection, while also counteracting white and yellow deodorant stains, and touted this accomplishment in the phrase: "black stays black, white stays white for longer."

Nivea worked with its consumers to gain fresh insights, create and innovate better products, and engage with consumers — everything millennials want.

With the help of its most valuable source of information, Nivea was able to please consumers in more than just one way.

This is what all companies need to start doing, if they haven't already done so. Looking at what a brand's consumers are saying is the best way to know what they want. Why keep guessing when information is available at your fingertips?

Beauty Tips:

- Millennials want a voice in what brands are doing to receive a more fun, personalized, and engaging consumer experience, so let them tell you what they want.
- Ask and listen. Turn to social media to learn what millennials want from your products and let them be a part of the creation process.
- Use co-creation as a method of interacting with your consumers and generating significant buzz about your brand.

- Co-creation is also an effective way to create value in the eyes of millennials by proving to them that brands are willing to tailor to the demands of their consumers.

CHAPTER 10

SHOW & TELL

——

"Design can be art. Design can be aesthetics. Design is so simple, that's why it is so complicated."

— PAUL RAND, AMERICAN ART DIRECTOR AND GRAPHIC
DESIGNER, BEST KNOWN FOR HIS CORPORATE LOGO
DESIGNS, INCLUDING THE LOGOS FOR IBM, UPS, ENRON,
MORNINGSTAR, INC., WESTINGHOUSE, ABC, AND NEXT.

Meg just got out of class for the day and needed to stop by CVS on her way home to pick up a few essentials that had been adding up on her list. She was out of shampoo and conditioner, so she needed to replenish her stock. Meg was looking to try something new. She had just finished her bottles of Garnier Whole Blends Repairing shampoo and conditioner her sister recommended, but didn't have as good of an experience as she would have liked.

She walked out the front gates of campus, past the colorful townhouses that lined O Street. She took the turn onto Wisconsin Avenue and walked into CVS to aisle two with all the hair products.

She carefully scanned the shelves, when a series of oval bottles with a gold cap caught her eye.

They were the Organix shampoos and conditioners. The colors drew her in closer and the simple text sold her on the packaging. The gold trim gave the products a luxurious feel, selling her on the fact that they had the potential of being high-quality products.

Meg looked closer at all the different options she had to pick from. Each bottle featured natural ingredients like biotin, tea tree oil, caffeine, lavender, bamboo fibers, and more.

As she was looking at all the products, Meg spotted a pretty light-colored bottle. She saw the word "coconut" on the label and figured she had to try it, since coconut is known to be hydrating. She knew her hair was relatively dry and straw-like, especially during spring when the humidity spikes up in D.C., leading her to give the product a try.

It was the simple packaging and the natural ingredients that sold Meg on the product. She has always been turned off by anything too distracting.

"I have always preferred simpler packaging without anything too flashy, like bright, flowery patterns. I would rather have my products be clean and sleek, since it shows that it is truly a quality product that doesn't need to rely on its flashiness to catch my attention. It tells me the product is more trustworthy and will perform," Meg said, reflecting on her product preferences.

**

A lipstick is a lipstick. You can have differences in shade, application, shine, or longevity, but, it'll typically come in a tube. Luckily, an easy way to make every lipstick different, is through the packaging.

According to research cited by The Paper Worker, one-third of consumer decision-making is based on packaging.

Packaging allows brands to create a visual point of difference. You can change the color, shape, size, or material, to create unique products that differentiates you brand from competitors.

It allows for an emotional selling point to stand out in a sea of products.

Brands first need to understand the consumer's point of view and know how to communicate to them. The best packaging is easy to understand and connects with consumers in a relevant way, while still aligning with the brand's values.

First things first, packaging needs to stand out. According to Business Insider, first impressions generally take about a split second, making all subsequent judgments based on quick information.

Meg's first impression of Organix happened in seconds, based on only the color and the design of the packaging. Before taking a closer look, she didn't even know the brand name.

At first glance, products need to draw consumers in and communicate the essence of the proposition. If consumers are scanning the shelves, the products are all going to blend together unless there is anything unique or noticeable that makes a product distinct from the others.

Christian Louboutin's Silky Satin Lip Colour does this perfectly. A blogger describes it as follows:

"The sales associate at the counter said that these are all hand-made, and it takes quite a while to make each case. The silky satin lip colors come packed in these gorgeous black boxes with velvet red interiors. Since these are satin-finish lipsticks, the cases have a shiny gold finish to them. They also come with these ribbons so that you can use these lipsticks as necklaces. Well, I would never do that but there is an option. The cover of the lipstick almost looks like a crown. It is colored in signature Louboutin red from the inside. They also come with little net covers that you can use while carrying the lipstick, which would prevent the lipstick from getting scratches. They are *so* stunning you'll want to carry them around with you all the time and flaunt them."

Louboutin's lipsticks exemplify being different and flashy. They resonate with consumers by swaying away from the norm. However, standing out from the crowd does have its challenges, since simplicity is usually more effective with packing.

So how do you find balance? It's all about knowing your brand and knowing who your consumer is.

Packaging can't be overwhelming. In a busy and visually agitated market, consumers rarely experience moments of sensory calm, which they tend to gravitate toward. This is a trend that is rising among millennials: they are gravitating towards minimalism, "white space," sans-serif fonts, and streamlined logos.

Herbivore Botanicals skincare is an all-natural, 100 percent plant based skincare company that formulates all of its products in small, handcrafted batches out of Seattle, Washington. The company doesn't use any fillers — only natural, safe, 100 percent vegan ingredients from nature.

Its products reflect who the company is, and so does its packaging. It's described as beautiful, minimal, and simple, just like the products. "The thoughtfully designed packaging and labels really allow the ingredients to shine through."

So it really depends on your brand. You could be Louboutin, who wants to stand out and attract its consumers through flashy and eye-catching packaging, or you could be like Herbivore Botanicals, who lets the products do the talking.

Millennials also seek experience. They are drawn to moments that appeal to their creative spirit. They want to be kept on their toes, seek adventure, and expect to find products that break the rules like they do. Most will even switch their brands and products for those that offer experiences. This presents the opportunity to tie experience into packaging.

It's important to consider how your packaging can create a sense of adventure for consumers. To do this, brands are creating interactive point-of-sales displays through augmented reality. Similar to Sephora, Shiseido offers its customers the option to try on makeup with the touch of a button. The use of the "try-before-you-buy" technology allows consumers to take a photo of themselves and apply makeup to the image. Consumers are seeking out this type of interactive experience.

Millennials also want a sense of ownership from their products. Not only do they want personalized experiences, but they also want to find individuality and differentiation in product packaging. They love having things that are unavailable to the rest of the world. This is why this generation has been leaning toward brands that offer them the option to create personalized packaging.

Coca-Cola successfully leveraged personalized packaging with its "Share a Coke" campaign. The campaign replaced the Coke logo on its cans with popular first names. By doing this, the company invited consumers to share a Coke with their friends and family members. Coke was even able to find ways around the fact that cans only had very generic names, like Sarah and Ron, which was especially crucial with the diversity within this generation.

Coke set up pop-up locations across the country where consumers could manually input the names they wanted to appear on a can into a machine, which would create a custom can right then and there. When I got the chance to do this, I was definitely more excited than I should have been. At first the Coke campaign didn't mean much to me because I knew "Kanika" would never appear on a can or bottle in a vending machine or in the grocery store. Having the opportunity to create my own can allowed to me create something that very few, if anyone, would have. To this day, I still have the can sitting on my desk.

This is very similar to Lancôme's personalized foundation. Its blend of products are custom-made for each individual and have a personalized unique code for each bottle that indicates that blend. The code is Lancôme's way of giving its packaging an individualized touch.

Now, with millennials, you can't forget about social media.

They love sharing their experiences with their networks and seeking out ways to interact with brands on their devices.

Many brands are leveraging this trend by finding ways of integrating social campaigns directly into their package designs. Coke was able to successfully expand on the "Share a Coke" campaign by encouraging its consumers to Tweet their own stories with the hashtag #ShareACoke. Not only did the campaign generate thousands of tweets, but it also gave Coke the opportunity to create sub-campaigns, like the campaign encouraging consumers to share a Tweet of a Coke product with the name "Ryan" on it be entered for a chance to meet and #ShareACoke with Ryan Seacrest.

Benefit Cosmetics did something similar by running it's #PoreOClock campaign. Michelle Stoodley, digital manager at Benefit Cosmetics, turned to social media to promote the company's new POREfessional Primer by creating the concept of "Pore O'Clock," which plays on the fact girls often need a makeup touch up at 4 P.M. "We decided to run a Twitter campaign with a 'we can come to you' CTA: 'tweet using #PoreOClock for a chance to win a visit from Benefit,'" where representatives handed out tubes of their POREfessional Primer. "We also ran a social sampling campaign. If you Tweeted #PoreOClock, it would automatically generate a personalized coupon that Twitter users could use to claim a sample of POREfessional stores. We ran this campaign throughout the month of January and it was very successful. We got tons of engagement: 17.5 thousand Twitter coupons were distributed, 38.8 thousand uses of #PoreOClock and it trended three times throughout the month."

Social media is one of the easiest ways to create buzz and ensure people are talking about your products. With this generation, it becomes a tool that should *always* be used anywhere possible, including on the packaging.

It's also important to note that millennials are environmentally conscious and value products that are natural and sustainable. Fifty-eight percent feel as though it is important for a brand to make them feel like a good person. Sixty-nine percent also agree that a brand that acts responsibly in the way it does business is also a key differentiator when making purchase decisions.

Herbivore Botanicals does this perfectly. It embraced its products and its mission of being all-natural by showcasing the clean, chic style of its eco-conscious packaging. "It feels green, but also very luxurious, in a way, and that's definitely something I look for in a natural beauty brand."

Blogger Door Sixteen said, "I don't want to stereotype too much here, but as someone who is increasingly doing a lot of shopping in health food stores' cosmetics aisles, I can tell you that vegan and natural are not usually words that I associate with incredible packaging design. And that stuff matters — it matters to me as someone who cares about design, and it matters when it comes to the perception of animal-friendly and natural products as being part of the world of luxury skin care." This shows just how important Herbivore Botanicals' packaging is to the product. The founders purposely crafted the packaging to reflect their values and missions, allowing the brand to reflect them in all aspects of the products.

We live in a world where everyone is always on the go. Most consumers don't have the time or energy to weigh the advantages and disadvantages of each and every product they are considering purchasing, so they use shortcuts to make their decision. Those shortcuts usually involve the packaging, which becomes the last type of media that consumers can't "screen out," meaning that no matter how they purchase the product, they will see the packaging in some shape or form. The best strategy is to incorporate the unique, personalized experiences and messages millennials crave into this unavoidable platform.

Beauty Tips:

- Millennials are influenced by packaging that reflects their own values, as well as the values of the brand. They want to be able to connect with the product in terms of how it portrays who they are as individuals.
- Millennials want interactive shopping experiences that are more engaging and creative at the point of sale.
- Millennials want packaging that is environmentally friendly and sustainable.

CHAPTER 11

BACK FOR MORE

"To millennials, loyalty programs are not just about freebies, but being part of a special club or experience. Members are willing to pay to get the extra benefits and feeling of being special."

— JASON DORSEY, A MILLENNIALS RESEARCHER AT THE CENTER FOR GENERATIONAL KINETICS.

On a bright sunny morning in the midst of summer, Meg was walking down Avenue des Champs-Élysées with her best friend Megan. Having just finished their petit déjeuner, the two were fueled with buttery croissants and fresh drip espressos.

Meg was on a mission. She had been a die-hard Sephora fan for years. Knowing that she was only in Paris for a couple days, the first item on her list was to visit the original flagship store that was established in 1996, which she knew gets even more visitors than the Eiffel Tower.

The sidewalks were crowded with both locals and tourists. The two girls were walking at a faster pace than everyone else, trying to make their way to the Sephora as fast as possible. They walked by H&M, MAC, and Levi's. Knowing they were getting closer with every step, they walked just a little bit faster.

When they made it to the front of the store, Meg stopped to take it all in. She was mesmerized. It was like walking into the beauty version of Willy Wonka's Chocolate Factory with the red carpet and a huge, luxurious bottle of J'Adore luring her inside. She had been waiting to take these first steps into the store since she first fell in love with makeup.

Despite the large size of the store, it was packed.

Meg and Megan slowly made their way in, pushing and shoving through the crowd until they got to the Urban Decay counter. This was the one brand Meg truly worshiped, so she knew she had to buy something. Meg was interested in a new blush and picked up Urban Decay's Afterglow in the color Bang.

A lovely French woman started assisting her. She was very accommodating and spoke English very well.

Meg asked her if she had any recommendations. The sales representative told her that the color was too dark for her and suggested the she try Score, a more suitable one for her skin tone. Meg was happy to receive her honest opinion over any brown-nosing.

The sales associate sat her down and applied the blush to her cheeks to show her how it would look. Meg was in love with the color and knew that she had to buy it right away.

She made her way to the checkout counter, where the line stretched for days, but she knew it was all worth it and part of the experience. When she got the the register, the cashier told her that she had enough Beauty Points to redeem an exclusive eyeliner that was only available in France. Meg didn't even wait for the cashier to ask her if she wanted to redeem her points; she jumped right in and said, "Oui! S'il vous plaît!"

Ecstatic to use her new blush and try out her new eyeliner, Meg kept browsing around while she waited for Megan to finish at the checkout. Meg loved being a rewards member but didn't realize it would ever get her such an exclusive product. She knew all her arguments with her parents about her excessive purchases at Sephora paid off — at least for her, but maybe not for her parents.

The two girls walked out of Sephora with their purchases

in hand, ready to explore the rest of what Paris had to offer.

**

I'm the person who walks into Starbucks and knows the barista by name. I go there for the coffee, not because I like the taste, but because I love the experience, community, and atmosphere of each store. I love ordering an Americano, finding a seat at a long table, and passing the afternoon doing work while listening to the soothing coffee shop songs. The sound of chatter and laughter blends with the background music that is at the perfect volume. The constant flow of people adds to the vibe of the place. Sitting in Starbucks and taking a sip of coffee gives me that warm, fuzzy feeling of sitting in the original location in Seattle on a cold, rainy day.

Millennials value experiences. They want to be part of an exclusive club and feel a sense of belonging to a brand's community. That is exactly what I am able to get by being a Starbucks Rewards member: a place in a coffee-loving neighborhood.

Now, I will admit, I am not a Gold member yet. I'm working my way up. Still, the real reason I love to go to Starbucks over other coffee chains is because of the atmosphere, experience, and community that I get, in addition to the good deals, like free refills and free food.

More and more loyalty programs are starting to incorporate experiential elements into their rewards, including VIP shopping events, exclusive access to products, and other opportunities that reflect what it's like to be involved in a brand.

If money is taken out of the equation, there are two things millennials value more than discounts: status at the company and the experiential rewards that strengthen their sense of being a VIP.

Sephora is a notable brand that has successfully been able to do this with its Beauty Insiders program

The name is where it all starts. These members automatically become part of the "Insider" community.

Sephora was the first loyalty program I was ever a part of. When I moved to Virginia, I went right into middle school, which I can't say were my glory days, but it was when I first got interested in buying and using makeup. Even though I was only in 7th grade, my friends were all wearing makeup to school. Naturally, I wanted to as well.

It all started with a trip to the mall with my mom. Tysons Corner in Virginia was one of the biggest malls I had ever been to. Walking in, I was overwhelmed by all the fast-paced people zooming past me. The mall I used to go to was never crowded, no matter what time or day I went.

My mom and I walked straight up to a map to try to get some sense of where we were in the sea of shops.

I had spotted Sephora on the map right away, but I hadn't mentioned to my mom that I wanted to buy any makeup because I knew she would say I was too young for it and I would "ruin" my skin. So we started off by just walking in and out of some stores. It was mostly window-shopping so we could get a sense of what the place was like and explore all the new brands we had never heard of before.

Eventually, we made our way past Sephora. I tapped my mom on the shoulder and asked her if we could stop in really quickly.

Walking into Sephora for the first time in your life when makeup is a whole new concept to you is even worse than walking to Walmart on Black Friday. People everywhere; makeup everywhere; and no clue where to take your next step.

A sales associate walked up and greeted me, but I was only 12 years old and very shy so I let my mom do all the talking. She told her we were just looking around and would let her know if we needed anything.

I walked away from my mom to where all the Sephora brand

products were placed. Their simple black packaging and neat display looked the least intimidating at the time. I picked up an eyeliner that said "Try Me" on it, and I drew a line on the back of my hand to test the first one. Then I got a little carried away and started trying all of them. After a few minutes, my hand ended up looking like a makeup bag had exploded on it. But I had to try everything — I was so fascinated by all the products and all the colors.

My mom walked over to my and told me we should leave, but I knew I couldn't go empty handed. I picked up one of the eyeliners that I liked the most and requested her to buy it for me. To my surprise, she was okay with that, but wanted me to first buy a smaller travel size to see if I actually did like it as much as I thought. She probably also wanted me to use it all up quickly so I would stop wearing it sooner, but I was more than happy taking anything she would give me. She found the sales associate to ask her if they carried a smaller version of the eyeliner and, luckily, they did.

We walked up to the register to check out. The cashier asked if we were Beauty Insiders. Since we just moved to the area, we weren't, and she offered to sign us up. I had heard my friends talking about the program for a while, telling me all about the free samples and free gifts they would get. I knew I wanted to be a part of it, especially at a time when I was just starting to explore the world of beauty. It was exactly what I needed. I nudged my mom's arm and begged her to sign up. She said no because she didn't want to have to manage another account, but I told her I would put my email down and take complete responsibility. After some whining, she finally agreed. I was so excited to be a part of the program and get all the benefits. It also gave me something else to talk about with my friends, which in the awkward middle school days was a huge plus, especially for the new kid.

The program itself gives members much more than free products and samples. Anyone can sign up and be a Beauty Insider to receive one point for every dollar spent in your Beauty Bank. Gather enough points, and you can use them on sample products from the "Rewards Bazaar". With 350 points, you become a Very Important Beauty (VIB) Insider, and get monthly gifts along with additional discounts. One thousand points is when things get interesting — these VIB Rouge Insiders, get free, limited-edition sets selected only for VIB Rouge members.

General membership entitles you to a free birthday gift, free in-store Sephora University beauty classes, select seasonal promotions, as well as access to special products and insider-only curated beauty sets. And work your way up to VIB or VIB Rouge to get access to exclusive events, access to pre-releases for specialty products, and as many free custom makeovers as you want.

Mallory is a VIB beauty member for Sephora's rewards system. "I share the account with my mom, so we both make purchases and put the points on our account. Then we tend to pretty evenly split the rewards. I would say we've been an insider for about three years. The best part is when I redeem points for some of the reward products. I love the feeling of getting a 'free' product every once in a while with my purchase. I also love that the rewards are mini product samples, because it allows me to try out new products that I wouldn't normally buy. The products are always relevant and good quality. There is often a lot of variety of products, too, so there always tends to be something I want to try. Every time I get the samples, I feel like I'm getting an exclusive membership gift that is specifically made for me. It's like I'm part of an exclusive beauty club that not many people are a part of!"

Not only do millennials seek status and experience, but they want to be loyal to brands that reflect their personalities. They expect brands to know them well — to know what they like, how they speak, and what they value the most.

Therefore, programs should reward millennials for what they love. This generation lives on social media, a medium companies can leverage by giving rewards for watching videos, posting on Instagram, sharing pages, downloading an app, or leaving a product review.

Le Pain Quotidien — which has the best avocado toast I've ever had — does everything through its mobile app, like Starbucks.

The LPQ app allows you to earn "dough," where one purchase is the equivalent of a piece of dough, and once you collect seven pieces, you get a coupon. The app allows you to keep track of all your purchases and rewards, lets you order ahead, and encourages social media sharing. Its "Spread the Love" feature allows users to tweet, text, or email their friends to "Spread the love and share the app with a friend. When your friend downloads the app and makes their first purchase, you'll receive one more piece of dough!"

This is an easy way for LPQ to get people talking about and downloading its app.

And LPQ isn't the only retailer to do this. There are many "refer a friend" promotions I hear about everywhere. It helps reward users for what they do best: talk and share!

Ulta Beauty has taken advantage of this. Each time a rewards member refers a friend who isn't already a member of the Ultamate Rewards program, they get a $10 off coupon and their friend gets $10 off the first Ulta Beauty purchase. Ulta's referral program encourages its members to share the program with others to get them to join, which is exactly what every retailer wants: more buzz and more customers.

Not only is this generation loyal to brands, but they are also loyal to causes. Thirty-nine percent are willing to do research into the sustainability efforts of companies before making a purchase and four out of five millennials say they are more likely to purchase from a company that supports a cause they care about.

MyCokeRewards fulfilled this desire perfectly. During its back-to-school campaign, Coca-Cola announced a sweepstake where participants could win a gift card worth $1,000. This not only created a fun way to get members involved and to generate buzz, but it also allowed members to give back to their favorite cause. Participants were able to choose a K-12 school that they wanted to support, to which Coke donated $1,000, just for the entry.

MAC does something similar on a consistent basis. The brand knows that consumers are going to keep using beauty products and are highly unlikely to completely cut out the use of cosmetics. Since product packaging creates a large amount of waste, MAC found a way to create a program that encourages consumers to recycle. Its Back-to-MAC Program allows consumers to bring back six empty containers of any type and receive a free lipstick in exchange. It's an effective way to reward consumers for buying their products, encouraging them to continue using the products, while also getting them to recycle to help the planet!

Although there are misconceptions that millennials are much less likely to be loyal to a brand, according to the Entrepreneur, 69 percent belong to a retail loyalty program and 68 percent are willing to change where they shop for more rewards.

It is clear these consumers are big on rewards and loyalty programs, not just for the discounts and price benefits, but also for the sense of community and power to give back. They want to connect with others who share similar interests.

Beauty Tips:

- This generation wants to be part of a club and gain status from the brands they are interacting with. Creating a loyalty program is an effective way to gather a community of loyal consumers and reward them for purchasing your products.
- Millennials want to do business with brands that support their values and beliefs. Align the values of your brand with your consumers', and reflect them through your rewards programs.
- Millennials want to support the causes they strongly believe

in. Centering your program around similar causes will create a larger incentive for these consumers to participate in them.

CHAPTER 12

FRESH FACE

———

"I now spend up to $500 every three to four months," he says. "Moisturizer daily, cleanser four days a week, face scrub three days a week, with my list of products geared toward my lifestyle."

— MARK TELLEY, 26-YEAR-OLD PROPERTY MANAGER.

On a cloudy London morning, Adam took a right off Commercial Street onto Brushfield Street until he found himself outside BarberBarber, a brand new gentleman's grooming salon that recently opened a location in Spitalfields Market.

Adam slowly opened the door. Upon walking in, he says he was "greeted by a member of staff who [guided him] downstairs to the hidden underground speakeasy, better known as 'The Dead Scoundrels Club'. The shop itself [was] a narrow but long salon with a combination of bright neon and polished steel that brings to mind images of American barbershops in the '50s. The dark wood walls and dark red leather chairs lead to a small cocktail bar with friendly staff behind, quietly making gin and whiskey cocktails for customers waiting to be served. A quiet hum of chatter and music greeted [him], alongside a Gin & Tonic, and [he] sat down with the newest edition of GQ waiting for [his] number to be called."

It wasn't long before Adam was greeted by two of the staff, Johnny and Joey. "Both were welcoming customers to the barber chairs and throwing around jokes that sparked bursts of laughter from other members of staff."

"It was enjoyable, fun and, most importantly, friendly. It was also barely midday, and I had just finished the Gin & Tonic…" Adam thought, taking a seat in front of a brightly lit mirror.

Joey asked Adam what he wanted done, and after a few minutes of consultation and playing around with his hair, the two of them settled on a look that Joey reassured he knew how to style. "This is a nerve-wracking point for anyone, to trust a stranger with your hair that you will then have to walk around with for the next few weeks. [Adam's] nerves were calmed after [Joey] washed [his] hair and started expertly trimming the back and sides."

"It was as professional as I've ever seen it in a London

barbershop," Adam reflected as he remembered his other experiences getting haircuts.

The two engaged in light conversation, chatting about what they do, who they are, etc. — typical dialog one can expect to have with their hair stylists. The chatter soon turned into banter as other stylists joined in, throwing a few jabs at each other's skills. It was all friendly competition.

Adam laughed and "watched as other customers indulged in a luxurious hot shave while the smell of cool menthol and sandalwood filled the shop. It was nothing short of a true pleasure to experience and be a part of."

"As [he] gathered [his] things and headed out the door, both Johnny and Joey shook [his] hand and said [he] needs to come back soon to catch up."

"There is a lot that can be said for a friendly face and warm goodbye," Adam thought to himself, as he walked out with a smile on his face.

**

Young male millennials are breaking out of the old, conventional stereotype about what it means to be "manly." Unlike their dads, these men are fairly comfortable with the idea of investing time and money into their personal care and daily routines. They are making a notable appearance in the professional grooming sector as avid and savvy users of grooming products and services, and as talented, forward-thinking grooming professionals, too.

Nathan Jancauskas, the founder of the high-end grooming store Men's Biz in Melbourne, says this is because "there is greater pressure on men to look their best today than at any time in recent history."

Fifty-two percent of male consumers consider their appearance to be either important or very important. Christian Courtin-Clarins, Chairman of Clarins, says, "The trend really began with sunscreens; even if they weren't convinced by other products, men got into the habit of protecting themselves in the sun. This convinced the beauty companies that there was a wider market for men's skin care."

Since I'm not really one to be able to speak to any of these claims about male grooming and their rise in the beauty and cosmetics industry, I had to start my search elsewhere.

I decided to begin my journey at Sephora. I walked down M Street in Georgetown until I saw the black and white-striped storefront. It was a Monday afternoon, so the store was barely crowded. As I entered I was greeted right away by a sales associate. She asked me if I needed any help and whether I was looking for anything specific. I asked her if the store carried any products that were specifically directed toward men. She led me up the stairs to the skin care department, which I was expecting, since I didn't know of many men, besides celebrities, who typically wore makeup. Once we got up, we walked around the stairs, and she lead me to two tiny shelves hidden away in the back of the store, with about 15 skin care products by Jack Black, supposedly the number one men's skin care brand — I had to Google the name to figure that out.

I asked the associate whether they had a lot of men coming into their store to purchase products. She told me she sees more men typically come in looking for gifts for their significant others, as opposed to for themselves.

I had been hoping to learn more about men's role in the beauty industry from Sephora, but I realized no man would want to walk into Sephora, where women are the target audience. Even though the company's website had a significant number of men's products, I was disappointed to see that its physical retail stores didn't as well.

With a little research, I found that when it comes to male products, 53.4 percent of males prefer to research and purchase their products from online stores, 18.7 percent prefer purchasing products from supermarkets, 9.3 percent favor beauty counters, and 8.4 percent prefer to research and purchase from male-based salons. The number one motivating factor that determines where men want to purchase their grooming products is convenience, especially the ability to purchase online. It is also important to keep in mind that most men prefer not to be seen at beauty counters, which are typically dominated by female consumers.

"The majority of men prefer to shop for toiletries in a self-selection environment. In many department stores, men's toiletry products are sold from the women's counter. However, men tend to find the idea of buying from a beauty consultant intimidating."

So I turned elsewhere.

I reached out to my brother, since I knew that there are some days when it takes him longer than me to get ready in the morning. To my advantage, he had already done similar research at his internship at the World Resource Institute.

I asked him: "What is your view on male grooming and the rising desire for males to take care of their appearance?"

He replied with the link to an article he helped research and write. This is what he had to say:

"It wasn't that long ago that the average Joe would tell you that using grooming products beyond hair gel and shaving supplies was flat-out taboo. But in recent years, male shoppers have increasingly turned to buying moisturizers, anti-aging creams and a host of other personal toiletries — to the point that the market for male grooming products is projected to be worth $19.5 billion in 2016. Sales of grooming products on one men's retail website increased 300 percent in 2015 alone."

"Companies selling grooming products have a deep understanding of the male consumer, and have used that knowledge to identify cues that reduce feelings of emasculation and may even help men feel more masculine when shopping for lotions and other items long seen as women's products. With names like "Facial Fuel" and "Urban Camouflage Concealer," products are now designed to readily appeal to the male consumer. They emphasize health and confidence as key benefits. Many are packaged in grey or black containers — even resembling cigars or liquor packaging — with bold typeface and few decorations. When sold in-store, companies maximize awareness by positioning the products in the men's section next to other accessories like belts."

"In short, companies and stores have realized ways to successfully introduce new grooming products to men, and many men have willingly adopted them. Gone are the days of one-size-fits all manhood, it seems. Even Axe, the body spray company that first made a name for itself with racy ads, has changed its tune, its advertising instead playing to the many different kinds of masculinity men are increasingly expressing."

I don't think I could have said it better myself.

It's clear that the sales pitch for men needs to be significantly different from that directed toward skin care-savvy women.

Elodie Bohuon, Selfridge's beauty buyer, says that "men are starting to get more and more knowledgeable about beauty and are paying attention to their looks: hair care is the biggest category, with shaving coming in second."

With constantly evolving hair trends, men are now seeking products that will serve them specifically, whether it's a clay pomade that's meant to keep hair neatly trimmed with a matte finish, or a hard water pomade for a light hold and a sleek shine.

But their spending doesn't just stop at hair and skin care. Much like women, men are also turning towards services — they are heading to salons for grooming, massages, and facials, as well as other treatments such as hair removal by waxing or laser. According to a survey by Salon Services, a professional beauty and hairdressing supplier, 25 percent of salon customers in 2015 were men.

Many see shaving and getting a haircut as regular, mundane chores, but there is a growing number of people who take pride in maintaining their appearance, and instead, see these as leisurely activities that they are willing to spend on.

Ever since my brother started going to a men's groomer for his haircuts, rather than the national chain he'd been going to for ever, he said he's been having a much better hair-cutting experience. The groomers are specially trained to cut men's hair, and he always likes the way his hair looks when he leaves. He said the best part of the whole service is the neck and shoulder massage they give at the end. "It's a nice and relaxing touch," he told me, as he walked through the door after coming back from his last haircut.

It's important to note that with all their purchase decisions, men tend to be more practical and efficient. They are careful about purchasing products that add too much extra time to their day-to-day routines and are a lot less influenced by marketing messages. Men, too, are looking for products that are compatible with their skin, but unlike women, they prefer fragrance-free products or more subtle scents.

High-end brand such as Estée Lauder, Kiehl's, and Clarins have had men's skin care products for years, and now we see more affordable lines, such as Everyman Jack grooming products, introduced by Target in 2007, and Dove's Men+Care, introduced in 2010. There are also subscription services such as Dollar Shave Club and Birchbox Man. These were created to specifically targeted the male millennial consumer.

When it comes to marketing products to millennial men, companies need to find ways to create the products men seek, while also being very careful about how they market them.

Selling cosmetics to men requires a completely different language than it does for women. Research shows that the second a man feels emasculated, the game is over. Since men are hesitant to associate with the concept of beauty, it's more impactful to speak to the health benefits of using a product.

Men also tend to view skin care as a solution to a problem, rather than as the pleasurable experience that women understand it to be. Male-centered skin care companies organize their websites around concerns like acne, wrinkles, and dry skin. It's all about the value proposition. Brands need to speak to their consumers in terms of a fix: you have a problem, we have a solution, and the solution works because it is backed up by science. Lab Series's Pro All-In-One Hydrating Gel "instantly draws in, retains, and locks in moisture to maintain hydration levels, while also calming and soothing the skin with an immediate cooling." Portland General Store has a

Face Bomb that is "nourishing to the face and provides a rustic and natural cleansing experience."

Brands are also making male consumers more comfortable by how they are naming their products. My brother mentioned Camouflage Concealer from the brand Mënaji, which combines the Scandinavian words for man and power. They also have a Lip Balm Agent that provides "vitamins for your lips."

Another important factor that men consider when purchasing skin care and cosmetic products is the packaging. Almost all men's skin care has minimalistic packaging with a brief description of what it promises to deliver. The goal is for the packaging to be simple and straightforward. They prefer more geometric shapes, such as squares and rectangles. They respond better to cooler tones and more aromatic colors like gray, blue, and black. Men also like graphics on packaging to help become more educated about products. Novel packaging helps brands differentiate themselves from their competition. For instance, Lab Series products come in simple white containers and include a little instruction booklet, much like the kind you'd find unboxing a radio or clock.

Men want their products to clearly communicate brand values, educate them on product benefits, and deliver on functionality. Like female millennials, men also want their brands to reflect their personality, create value and a tactile experience, and most importantly, tell a story.

Millennial men are becoming increasingly open-minded about grooming practices and routines. They want to take care of their appearance and present themselves well to others. To truly reach and speak to this market, brands need to update their marketing techniques to reflect their customer bases.

Beauty Tips:

- Male millennials have a significantly growing market share in the beauty industry. Brands can't forget about this influential group and need to start speaking to them more meaningfuly.
- These consumers prefer shopping online, since it is more convenient and allows them to avoid the female-centric and women-dominated beauty counters.
- Male shoppers are concerned about emasculation. They will be turned off if a brand threatens their strength and power.
- To male millennials, skin care and beauty products are seen as solutions to problems. They want their products presented in a way that states how the product benefits are backed by science.
- Male millennials want their packaging and product name to be as distinguished from female products as possible. They look for simplicity and the ability for the products to reflect their personality, value, and identity.

- Like their female counterparts, male consumers are also seeking an experience that tells a story.

CHAPTER 13

EVERLASTING BEAUTY

———

"Millennials are leading a change in purchase trends."

— RODNEY MASON, GLOBAL VICE PRESIDENT
OF MARKETING AT BLACKHAWK ENGAGEMENT SOLUTIONS.

The customer is always right. We've all heard that saying, and it is particularly true of millennial customers. They need to believe it if they are to continue purchasing your product. Millennials are the most powerful and influential customers the world has seen. In an industry projected to grow to $51.8 billion by 2020, listening to millennials is crucial to any brand's success. Marketers need to remember this and learn how to effectively use it to their advantage.

The main takeaways of millennials' values, beliefs, and preferences towards the beauty industry are:

"Testing is vital to today's consumers."

I want to be able to test out the products that I'm buying before investing in them with a swipe of my credit card or click of a button. The millennial "try-before-you-buy" mentality is now stronger than ever. They want to know that their products deliver on quality and are worth purchasing.

"As a group with a penchant for self-expression and individualism, millennials like choice."

These consumers want choice, individualism, and personalization. They want their brands and products to be perfectly tailored to who they are as unique individuals. They want brands to speak to them as individuals to create lasting, loyal relationships.

"Most purchases are planned — consumers now go in knowing what they want at least 70 percent of the time."

I don't remember the last time I window-shopped for beauty and cosmetic products. For the most part, I usually have a reason to be at a retailer or on a retailer's website. I prefer to explore online for products with the help of blogs and product reviews. Then I go to the physical stores, already knowing what I intend to buy. I don't use my in-store visit to browse, but rather as an opportunity to try the products to see if they uphold the expectations created by my research.

But it doesn't stop there. Surely, a lot more change is bound to come because of innovation and technology, which will create new "must-have" products.

The ability to customize experiences and products will only continue to grow, with the rise of make-your-own palettes and other skin care, hair-care, fragrance, and makeup products that allow for consumer personalization and involvement.

Imagine stepping into Sephora one day. The app on your phone detects that you're in the store and automatically sends you a push notification with a list of product recommendations based both on your app profile, which covers basics like your skin type and skin tone, and your past purchases. You can click each item on the app to get a product description and a map directing you to where the product is located in the store.

You walked into Sephora with the intention of only buying more avocado face masks, but you decide to follow the map to the Tom Ford Lip Color lipsticks. The app recommended you the shade Satin Finish. You try it on and like it, but not enough to be convinced to buy it. You keep browsing through the other colors and pick up Forbidden Pink. You try that one on too and like it a little better than the previous one.

But something in you tells you to try mixing the two colors together.

You layer the two shades, one on top of the other, and rub your lips together to make sure the colors are mixed thoroughly. You look at yourself in the mirror and fall in love with the color. You know you have to wear that shade out to dinner the next night, but you don't want to have to buy both shades, since they are $53 each and you know you can barely afford one.

Lucky for you, Tom Ford allows you to make your own colors. You take both shades up to the sales associate and tell her you want a 50/50 mix of each color in one tube. She writes down the two colors and the mix you want on a form, and tells you to follow her to the back counter to a shiny machine. The associate pulls out both colors from a drawer filled with tubes of lipsticks lined alongside each other.

She places the two in a machine that cuts off equal parts of the product from each tube. The machine melts and swirls the colors together and lets the new shade drip down into a mold attached to a new tube. The associate picks up the mold and places it in a blast chiller for 30 seconds to let it cool. She pulls it out, places a sticker with tiny numbers and letters on the bottom of the tube with "KM - 50-1917293/50-1917046," which represents your initials, the percent blend of each original color, and the item number of each original color.

The associate hands you the new personalized lipstick, and just like that, you are the creator of your own original shade of Tom Ford lipstick.

Although this is not a reality now, I know one day it will be.

On top of that, the demand for natural formulas, sustainability, and information about ingredient safety will most likely continue to increase, so you'll start seeing more and more products that work in response to these demands and fewer ones that use harsh added chemicals — maybe even give consumers the ability to pick which ingredients they want in their face wash or moisturizer.

For the most part, buying will most likely stay in the physical world rather than online, giving consumers more control and opportunities to test, try, and learn before they buy.

"The hope is that this all leads to more extensive results-testing, more transparency, and, finally, more effective products," says Beth Shapouri, freelance content specialist and former lead beauty writer for Glamour.com. As millennials continue to dominate the beauty space, products that are able to deliver on the promises they make and live up to the hype created by social media, advertising campaigns, and digital and social

communications, will become one of the most important influencers on consumers.

It's safe to say that millennials have created a new language
of beauty. Now, you as a marketer know how these
consumers are different from previous generations, know
what they want, and know how they want it. With these tools
under your makeup belt, you have the knowledge and
understanding you need to truly resonate with this group
of influential consumers. You are now not only equipped
to understand the language millennials speak, but to also
become fluent in it yourself. And this fluency will allow
you to change the future of marketing.

ACKNOWLEDGEMENTS

I would like to thank everyone who helped me turn this book a reality. It wasn't an easy process, but words cannot describe how grateful I am and how fortunate I am to be a published author.

I want to give a special shoutout to everyone who let me interview them, sharing their insights and words of wisdom. All my friends, who understood why there were days I choose my book over them. Yasmeen, who replied to all the texts and questions in a matter of minutes at any time of day. Anastasia, who gave me amazing feedback throughout the whole process. Emma, for completely editing my book in such short notice. Brian, for guiding me through the publication process. Eric, for giving me this incredible opportunity. And finally, my parents and brother, who kindly offered me their help whenever I needed it.

I would not have been able to accomplish this without any of you.